RMS Queen Mary Manual

Gary Chambers

"The Queen Mary, launched today, will know its greatest fame and popularity when she never sails another mile and never carries another passenger."

Lady Mable Fortescue-Harrison (Astrologer), 1934

Contents

Foreword

Over the past eight decades, many words have been written and spoken about the former Cunard liner, R.M.S. *Queen Mary*. Since her inception and troubled birth from the ruins of the Great Depression, this remarkable vessel has had somewhat of a providential kiss upon her noble life. It's a wonder she was even completed at all. Surely the risks taken in the Second World War to sail her packed with thousands of GI's across dangerous u-boat infested waters, only to arrive close to shores where bombers were waiting to blast her into eternal blue, was extraordinary in the history of seafaring. And finally, after 31 years of matchless seagoing service and 3.8 million nautical miles traveled, the *Queen Mary* would escape the ship breakers hammer and begin a new life as a floating Southern California icon.

I love to think of her dazzling speed on those Blue Riband crossings in her glamour years before the war when she was known the world over as Britain's masterpiece. She had become perhaps the most prosperous liner on the North Atlantic route. Certainly her service as a troop carrier remains unparalleled. All of us today enjoy the fruits of the peace and the freedoms from Nazi tyranny that were so vastly influenced by the *Queen Mary*.

I love to marvel also at the glory days between 1947 and 1957 when the *Queen Mary* and *Queen Elizabeth* reigned as the supreme expressions of ocean travel, sailing with full passenger loads every voyage, earning what they cost to build every year. The *Mary*, of course, seemed to be the preferred ship with passengers and crew alike. Again, something almost preordained or even supernatural.

After soldiering on for ten years following the dawning of the jet age, the *Queen Mary* would be retired and sold to the City of Long Beach California in 1967. The enormous dowager liner would arrive in her new home 39 days 14,500 miles out from Southampton England on December 9th that same year. She remains to this day a testament to the Scottish shipbuilding arts and the British Merchant Navy. These days Cunard Line operates a modern fleet of three ships with classic 'Queen' branding. They are magnificent indeed, especially the *Queen Mary 2*, a billion dollar namesake built to emulate and carry the proud traditions and exquisite service of their first *Queen Mary*. This is unprecedented in the annals of ocean travel.

Although the *Queen Mary* no longer sails, her popularity remains unabated. An estimated 55 million people have visited the ship in Long Beach since opening in May of 1971 as a hotel, attraction and place for special events. More than 10 thousand weddings have been performed onboard the majestic liner!

There are 10 million rivets holding the *Queen Mary* together, and I believe for every one of those rivets, there is a heart somewhere in the world the great ship touches. Gary Chambers is one of those millions of hearts. Thankfully, he has harnessed his time and energy to create this wonderful and very informative book of facts and lore for us all to enjoy. He not only speaks of the *Queen Mary's* illustrious past, but also her very beaming, vibrant present. Many thanks, Gary, from all of us who share your great admiration for the *Queen of hearts.*

I can attest that the *Queen Mary* is very much a ship with a soul. Her robust character and unique longevity fascinates even me as she has dominated my life for some 40 years. Perhaps King George V spoke her soul into her with his words on the day of the launching in September 1934 when he said, "No longer will she be a number on the books, but a ship with a name in the world, alive with beauty, energy and strength." We may never know exactly what it is that makes the *Queen Mary* what she is to the human heart and psyche, but I think that it is safe to say, "there is something about *Mary!*"

Maria Regina in saecula saeculorum!!!
(Queen Mary unto the ages)

Commodore Everette Hoard
(Honorary)
R.M.S. Queen Mary
March 20, 2019
at Long Beach

Introduction

Explore the incredible history and operation of the *RMS Queen Mary* as we take an up close look at how this beloved classic transatlantic ocean liner actually worked. Learn about the design, construction, operation and extensive safety features of one of the most famous ships ever constructed. Detailed explanations, photographs and illustrations show how the *Queen Mary's* systems actually worked, how the esteemed Captain and officers skillfully operated and navigated this majestic ship across expansive oceans, and all about the exquisite art deco passenger accommodations and facilities from the golden age of travel.

In addition learn how the ship's magnificent spaces were forever changed during her conversion to a premiere hotel and tourist attraction for her retirement in beautiful Long Beach, California.

History

The *Queen Mary* was initially known as 'Number 534' the job number given to her by the shipyard John Brown & Company Ltd. whose shipyard was in Clydebank, Scotland. Construction on the *Queen* started on 1 December 1930 but stopped after a year due to the Great Depression. On 30 December 1933 the British Government agreed to provide a loan to complete the *Queen Mary* and construct her sister ship *RMS Queen Elizabeth* on condition that the shipping lines Cunard and White Star Line merged. Work restarted on the *Queen Mary* on 3 April 1934. The companies merged on 10 May 1934 and the Cunard-White Star Line was formed.

Her name *Queen Mary* came from the real Queen Mary (wife of King George V.) who christened the ship at the launch on 26 September 1934, where King George V. called her the "Stateliest Ship in Being."

After her interiors were fitted, on 27 May 1936 she sailed on her maiden voyage from Southampton to Cherbourg and onwards to New York commanded by Sir Edgar T. Britten, the date chosen to coincide with the actual Queen Mary's birthday. With a speed of 29.13 knots she took 4 days, 5 hours and 46 minutes to cross the Atlantic (measured from Cherbourg, France to the Ambrose Light Vessel off New York) arriving on 1 June 1936.

In August 1936 the *Queen Mary* set a speed record crossing the Atlantic (2,939 nautical miles) in 3 days, 23 hours and 57 minutes at a speed of 30.63 knots, whereupon she won the esteemed 'Blue Riband' award. Despite losing the award in 1937 to the *Normandie* (French ocean liner) the *Queen* won it back the following year when she set an even faster record in August 1938 making the crossing in 3 days, 20 hours and 42 minutes, at a speed of 31.69 knots. She held the award until 1952 when the *SS United States* set a new faster record.

(Above) *Queen Mary* welcomed as she arrives in New York, completing her maiden voyage, on 1 June 1936.

When the Second World War broke out the *Queen Mary* and later the *Queen Elizabeth* were requisitioned as troopships and sailed to Australia for conversion, they were repainted in Navy gray. Owing to her speed and grey exterior the *Queen* was referred to as the "Gray Ghost." After conversion she carried Australian and New Zealand soldiers to the United Kingdom to fight in the war. The *Queen* carried over 15,000 solders at a time, with such an impact on the war effort Hitler placed a $250,000 bounty and an Iron Cross with Oak Leak Cluster for any U-Boat commander that sank her, putting her at risk from U-Boats. To confuse the U-Boats she sailed in a zig-zag pattern, however, on 2 October 1942 while maneuvering she accidentally sliced through and sank one of her escort ships, the *HMS Curacoa*. Despite a damaged bow the *Queen* was under strict orders and was not permitted to stop which would have put thousands of lives onboard at great risk. Three hundred and thirty eight died in the collision.

Still holding the Blue Riband award, another record was broken (25-30 July 1943) when the *Queen Mary* carried 15,740 soldiers, the most passengers to date on any vessel. Throughout the war the *Queen* sailed 661,771 miles and carried 810,730 military personnel. In addition to soldiers, the *Queen Mary* also carried 19,000 war brides, and 4,000 children, forever changing people's lives.

When the war was over, the *Queen Mary* was refitted and put back into transatlantic service, however, crossing the Atlantic by ship suffered a downturn when transatlantic jet travel became a reality in 1958, reducing the journey from days, down to hours. Now operating the ship at a loss, and with more modern and cost effective ships sailing, the *Queen Mary* was retired in 1967.

Saved from the breakers, the *Queen Mary* found a home in Long Beach, California, whose City purchased the ship for $3.45 million to use her as a permanently moored hotel and tourist attraction.

In-order to deliver the ship to Long Beach, rather than sail it empty at a loss, a final voyage was organized commanded by Captain Treasure Jones (who himself retired after this voyage). The voyage required sailing around Cape Horn, as she was too wide for the Panama Canal.

On arrival she was converted into a hotel and tourist attraction and opened to the public on 8 May 1971. During her time at sea she carried 2,114,000 fare paying passengers and sailed 3,794,017 nautical miles!

Thanks to the City of Long Beach, guests and visitors alike are able to continue to stay-on and appreciate the on-going legacy of the *RMS Queen Mary*.

Timeline

December 1, 1930	Keel laid
December 10, 1931	Work suspended
April 3, 1934	Work resumed
September 26, 1934	Launched
March 24, 1936	Departed Clydebank
April 15-19, 1936	Sea Trails
May 12, 1936	Officially handed over to owners
May 27, 1936	Maiden voyage
March 1, 1940	Requisitioned for war service
October 2, 1941	Collided with *HMS Curacoa*
July 31, 1947	Return to service after war
1958	Stabilizers fitted
September 19, 1967	Retired
October 31, 1967	Departure of Last Great Cruise
December 9, 1967	Arrived in Long Beach
May 8, 1971	Opened as a museum and tourist attraction.

Specifications

Builder: John Brown & Company Ltd.
(Clydebank, Scotland)

Yard Number: 534
Gross Tonnage: 80,773 tons (increased to 81,237 tons)
Over 10,000,000 rivets used in construction
Over 2,000 portholes and windows (2,500 sq. ft. of glass)

Length: 1,019 ft. (1,004 ft. at waterline)
Beam (Width): 118 ft.
Draft: 39 ft. 4 9/16 inches

Boiler rooms: 5
Boilers: 24 Yarrow water-tube boilers & 3 Scotch boilers

Number of passengers: 2,139 (1936)
Officers & Crew: 1,174
War time capacity: 16,683 (15,740 soldiers and 943 crew)

Number of cabins: 949
Number of telephones: 600
Number of electric clocks: 700

Cost (1930s) around $10,000,000

Design

To design the *Queen Mary* her builders, John Brown & Co., Ltd. conducted around eight thousand experimental tests, using twenty two ship models in their own enormous water tank (400 ft. long by 20 ft. wide) to create the final design of the *Queen Mary*.

Almost one thousand experiments with model propellers were conducted in both the water tank and in open water to develop the propellers shape, and a wind tunnel was even used to help determine the height and shape of the funnels.

Twelve decks were incorporated, of those A Deck and the four below travel the length of the ship uninterrupted. Heavy engines and machinery were positioned in gigantic spaces in the lower decks which increased the stability of the ship.

The sleek, beautiful design was synonymous of the classic ocean liners, with graceful curvature of the hull called sheer. With sheer the bow majestically curves up high out of the water, while the aft end curved to a lower height. This curvature increased buoyancy and prevented the ends from diving into powerful waves at sea, which would have caused the ship to slow down, it also reduced the mighty Atlantic Ocean's waves ability to wash across the decks. The sheer design can readily be seen on A Deck where the floor curves up at the ends.

(Above) A Deck's floor curves up in the distance and illustrates the hull's sheer, which protected the ship against ocean waves. Bakelite handrails (early plastic) were added after a few voyages.

Decks & Notable Features

Navigation Bridge & Compass Platform	Bridge
Sports Deck	Deck Officers' Quarters, Deck Tennis Courts, Dog Kennels, Funnels
Sun Deck	Cabin Class Gymnasium, Cabins, Squash Court, Lifeboats, Verandah Grill
Promenade Deck	Observation Bar, Cabin; Music Studio, Lecture Room, Library, Main Hall & Shopping, Writing Rooms, Main Lounge, Long Gallery, Ballroom, Starboard Gallery, Smoking Room, Tourist; Smoking Room, Mermaid Bar
Main Deck	Garden Lounge, Cabin Travel Bureau, Staterooms & Suites, Tourist; Main Lounge, Library & Writing Room, Playroom
A Deck	Cabin Staterooms & Suites, Tourist; Cabins, Overflow Lounge, Third; Smoking Room, Barber Shop & Beauty Parlor, Cabins
B Deck	Cabin; Staterooms, Barber Shops & Beauty Parlor, Tourist; Barber Shop & Beauty Parlor, Cabins, Synagogue, Third; Playroom, Cinema, Library, Cabins, Crew Quarters, Isolation Wards
C Deck (now R Deck)	Cabin Dining Room, Kitchens, Pool & Turkish Baths, Tourist; Entrance, Dining Saloon, Cabins, Third Dining Saloon, Cabins, Crew Quarters

D Deck (now C Deck)	Cabin Swimming Pool & Turkish Baths, Tourist & Third Cabins, Crew Quarters
E Deck (now D Deck)	Tourist & Third Cabins, Crew Quarters
F Deck (now E Deck)	Tourist Swimming Pool & Gymnasium, Baggage & Cargo Holds
G Deck (now F Deck)	Tourist Swimming Pool & Gymnasium, Baggage & Cargo Holds, Linen Stores, Cherbourg Mailrooms
H Deck (now G Deck)	Cargo Holds, Generators, Water Softening Plant, Boilers, Engine Rooms & Propellor Shafts
Tank Tops & Hull	Cargo Holds, Water Ballast

Construction

The *Queen Mary* was constructed by John Brown & Company Ltd., in Clydebank, Scotland, located to the northwest of Glasgow along the River Clyde.

(Above) Fore end of the *Queen Mary* taken from the west crane at John Brown & Co's Shipyard at Clydebank.

Massive frames and girders created a skeleton on to which huge steel sheets (shell plates) were riveted using pneumatic hammers to form the hull. The plates were between 8 and 36 ft. long and many over 6 ft. wide.

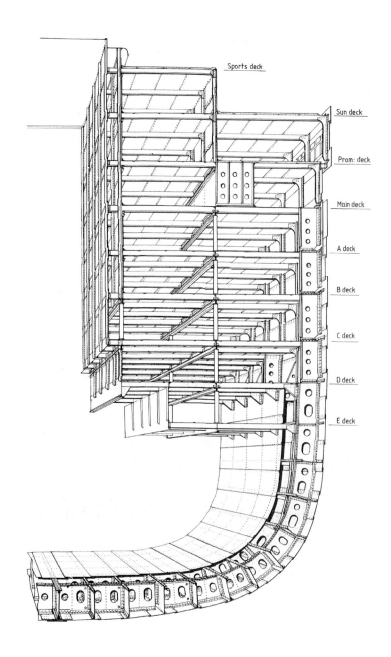

Sports deck

Sun deck

Prom: deck

Main deck

A deck

B deck

C deck

D deck

E deck

(Above) Section of the *Queen Mary's* steel frame, the double bottom can be seen extending high up the side.

Over ten million rivets made of ingot steel held the plates together, they varied in length and were between 2 and 4 1/2 inches long. The rivets alone weighed 4,000 tons and would have extended 270 miles if placed end to end.

(Above) *Queen Mary* on the wharf at John Brown & Company's shipyard, Clydebank.

The weight of the stern frame shaft brackets and rudder weighed almost 600 tons, while the hull and machinery weighed over an incredible 50,000 tons!

(Above) *Queen Mary* pictured during her sea trials.

There was plenty of wood used too, around 1,000 tons of the hardwood Burma teak (*Tectona Grandis*) was used on decks and for other needs.

A 1,200 ft. long by 135 ft. wide dry dock was built in Southampton, called 'King George V Graving Dock,' it held 58 million gallons of water! Before the maiden voyage the ship was dry docked here and made ready, costing the builders £6,000 to use the dock.

(Above) *Queen Mary* leaving Clydebank Dock.

(In 2005 the King George V Graving Dock's lock gate was removed converting it into a permanent wet dock. The following year the dock's historical importance to the age of transatlantic liners was recognized when it became a listed building.)

Sailing Routes

The *Queen Mary* was built to cross the North Atlantic Ocean, along with her sister ship the *RMS Queen Elizabeth*. The ships provided weekly service between Southampton, Cherbourg and New York. To maintain such an express service the ship could arrive in port, disembark her two thousand or more passengers, refuel, embark new passengers and proceed on to the next voyage within twelve hours if needed.

Accommodating these colossal ships required massive docks. In New York a new 1,100 ft. long pier ('Pier 90') was constructed on the west side of Manhattan on the Hudson River, at a cost of £2,000,000 and rented for £48,000 per year. Pier 90 was part of Luxury Liner Row, a group of four docks (Piers 88-94) that historically accommodated the classic ocean liners. Across the Atlantic in Southampton the *Queen Mary* docked at the 'Ocean Dock' this was complimented in 1950 with a new terminal ('Ocean Terminal') to handle the large numbers of passengers traveling on ocean liners, including the *Queen Mary*.

Over the course of thirty one years, the *Queen Mary* crossed the Atlantic Ocean one thousand and one times!

(The Manhattan Cruise Terminal is now located on Pier's 88 and 90. Pier's 92 and 94 are used for event space. The Ocean Terminal was demolished in 1983.)

Passenger Accommodation

Each voyage had three classes of travel based on the cost of the ticket; Cabin, Tourist and Third Class.

	Capacity (1936)	Capacity (1957)	Cost of Return Ticket
Cabin Class (1st)	776	711	£110
Tourist Class (2nd)	784	707	£56
Third Class	579	577	£37 10s 0d

Cabin arrangement (by class) was based on comfort (ships pitching moment at sea) therefore Cabin Class rooms were in the middle of the ship, Tourist Class were furthest aft and Third Class rooms were the furthest forward. Each class had their own entrance and public rooms that were grouped around their own staircase, thereby creating separate sections for each class. In 1948 the class names were changed as can be seen in the table below.

Queen Mary's Class Names (before and after 1948):

	1936-1947	1948 Onwards
(1st Class)	Cabin Class	First Class
(2nd Class)	Tourist Class	Cabin Class
(3rd Class)	Third Class	Tourist Class

18

Public Rooms by Class

Cabin Class (1st)	Tourist Class (2nd)	Third Class (3rd)
Restaurant & Foyer	Dining Saloon	Dining Saloon
Main Lounge	Tourist Class Main Lounge & Overflow Lounge	Garden Lounge & Lounge
Smoking Room	Smoke Room	Smoke Room
Library	Library	Books available in Cinema and Lounge
Ball Room	-	-
Writing Room	Writing Room	-
Observation Lounge & Cocktail Bar	-	-
Children's Room	Children's Room	Children's Room
Verandah Grill	-	-
Swimming Pool	Swimming Pool	-
Turkish & Curtive Baths	-	-
Gymnasium	Gymnasium	-
Squash Rackets Court	-	-

Cabin Class Staterooms

Cabin Class Staterooms (1st class) were located on the Sun Deck, Main Deck and A and B Decks. These rooms were single and two berth cabins, most of them were on the outside with portholes for light and air, with combined bedroom / sitting room and private bathroom.

(Above) Modern day use of a Cabin Class Stateroom.

A number of cabins were suites and had a bedroom, sitting-room, servant's room, box-room and private bathroom.

The portholes were opened and closed by bedroom stewards to provide fresh air, and passengers had an electric fan and Punkah Louvre to control air temperature (form of air conditioning) as well as having an electric heater.

(Above) Mock-up of a cabin class sitting-room.

Each stateroom also had wardrobes, dressing tables and chairs and a clock and lights. There was also an electric clock which like all the clocks onboard were 'repeaters' from the master chronometer in the chartroom.

The private bathrooms had hot and cold fresh water as well as salt-water. The bath came with a fitted shower attachment.

Conversion Notes: The staterooms are substantially unchanged, however, the (direct current) fans no longer work as the ship is now powered by alternating current.

Tourist Class Cabins

Tourist Class Cabins (2nd Class) were spread over five decks (A to E Deck) and were between two and four berths. The upper berths had folding Pullman type beds.

(Above) Tourist class cabin (A-210) with Pullman bed on right.

Most of the rooms were outboard and had a private bathroom with the majority also having a toilet. In the cabins where easy chairs, settees and wardrobes.

Conversion Notes: All tourist class cabins were removed, those on A and B Decks were reconfigured as larger cabins for hotel rooms and are not original to the ship.

Third Class Cabins

Third Class Cabins were either two or four berths, with an upper berth of the folding Pullman type creating a similar look of a bunkbed.

(Above) Mock-up of a third class cabin.

The rooms came with a washbasin, hardwood wardrobe, dressing table. chairs and stools. Like in the other types of cabin there was also an electric fan.

Conversion Notes: All third class cabins were removed. An exhibit on the ship (shown above) provides a sense of what these cabins and furnishings were like.

Artwork

The *Queen Mary* is a treasure trove of artwork, it can be found almost everywhere onboard. Over thirty talented artists skillfully enhanced the ship with art in multiple forms, from beautiful paintings, detailed glass etchings to stunning wood marquetry and intricate carvings.

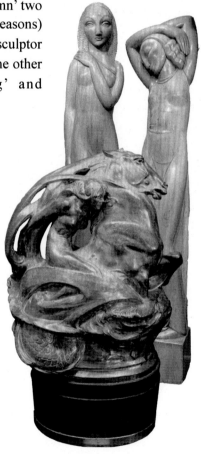

(Right) 'Summer' and 'Autumn' two of four statuettes (Four Seasons) carved in lime-tree wood by sculptor Norman Forrest (b. 1898.) The other two statuettes ('Spring' and 'Winter') were lost.

(Below Right) 'The Sea King's Daughter' by English sculptor Gilbert Bayes (1872-1953). This bronze statue was originally one of four originally found in the Cabin Class Main Lounge, Promenade Deck.

Conversion Notes: Artwork can be viewed in the original location, other pieces were moved and are on display elsewhere on the ship.

Woods

The *Queen Mary* was known as the 'Ship of Woods' with nearly sixty different types of wood used onboard. Six types of wood used are now extinct.

(Above) A promotional exhibit illustrates the various wood veneers used on the ship. Behind the exhibit are the starboard lift doors (elevators) on the Promenade Deck.

Wood is purposely used throughout the ship to set the tone for almost every space, mixing texture, grain and wood color to accentuate walls with a richness only possible with this wonderful natural material. Clever use of different wood types may not be apparent at first, but have been used to great effect throughout the ship.

Wood Veneers On-Board

Amboyna	Honduras Mahogany	Pine
Australian Maple (Warri)	Hornbeam	Plain Teak
Avodire	Indian Gold Padouk (Burma Padauk)	Pomele (a figured Mahogany)
Beech	Indian White Mahogany (Dhup)	Queensland Maple
Bird's Eye Maple	Japanese Ash (Tamo	Quilted Maple
Brazilian Peroba	Japanese Chestnut	Red Cedar
Brown Curly Oak (English Oak)	Light Oak Burr	Rosewood
Bublinga (African Rosewood)	Macassar Ebony	Sapele Mahogany
Burr Ash	Makore (African Cherry)	Silky Oak
Canadian Birch	Masur Birch	Silver Maple
Chestnut	Moselle figured Birch	Swedish Birch
Coral color Mahogany (Agha)	Mountain Ash	Thuya Burr (Citron Wood)
Elm Burr	Natural White Sycamore (Harewood)	Walnut
English Brown Ash	Nigerian Pommel	Weathered Sycamore

English Figured Beech	Oak	White Ash
English Oak	Oaknut (English Chestnut)	White Birch
Figured Cherry	Olive Wood	Yew
Figured Maple	Patapsco (Figured Maple)	Zebrano (Zebrawood)
Figured Teak	Pearwood	Pine
Golden Ash	Petula (a variety of Birch)	Plain Teak

Shops

Main Hall & Shopping Centre

The Main Hall & Shopping Centre on the Promenade Deck was a popular shopping area known as 'Bond Street,' that was 90 ft. long.

(Above) Main Hall looking forward.

This was a central area for cabin class passengers and offered a clothing, tobacco and book store, a Library, Drawing Room, Writing Rooms and telephone kiosks. Forward of the Main Hall where other public rooms including a Lecture Room, Music Room, children's Playroom and Observation Bar.

Originally the Main Hall's flooring had a bold art deco design with wide colored stripes, however, this was replaced after the war and once again since.

At the fore end of the hall was a store (originally an Austin Reed clothing store) with a 50 ft. long ivory tone plaster frieze entitled 'Sport and Speed' by Mr. Maurice Lambert (1901-1964).

(Above) Inside the former Austin Reed store.

On the after end of the Main Hall was a staircase that led to the cabin class areas. Mounted on the wall at the head of the staircase (behind which was a funnel shaft) was a marble medallion plaque of Her Majesty Queen Mary, by Lady Hilton Young (Lady Kennett) (1878-1947).

(Above) Replica medallion plaque of Her Majesty Queen Mary, which replaced the original marble plaque.

Displayed proudly below the plaque was the 'standard,' a flag presented to the ship by Her Majesty.

Conversion Notes: The marble medallion plaque of Her Majesty Queen Mary was replaced with a replica. The flag was moved to the Queen Elizabeth 2. The shopping area was renamed to 'Piccadilly Circus' and the stores now sell a variety of Queen Mary branded products and other interesting items.

Restaurants

Cabin Class Dining Room

The Cabin Class Dining Room was located on C Deck (now R Deck) and was the largest room onboard measuring 143 ft. long and spanning the width of the ship. The room's large space created grandeur at 18,730 sq. ft. In the central area of the room the tiered ceiling rises a stunning 27 ft., extending through A and B Decks above. The vast Dining Room could seat eight hundred and fifteen diners at a time (all of the cabin class passengers). Originally the flooring was Korkoid linoleum (linoleum layer on a cork base) laid with a diagonal square tiled pattern.

(Above) Looking forward from the starboard side.

(Above) Atlantic Map, by Mr. MacDonald Gill.

On both ends of the room were stunning pieces of art, on the fore end of the dining room was a colossal map of the North Atlantic Ocean (24 ft. wide by 15 ft. tall) by Mr. Leslie MacDonald Gill (1884-1947) behind which was a funnel shaft. An illuminated crystal model of the *Queen Mary* moved across one of two tracks on the map to show the ship's current position across the Atlantic Ocean, the track used represented either the summer or winter track depending on time of year. Mounted opposite on the after end is a painting in tapestry technique entitled 'Merrie England' by English artist Mr. Philip Connard (1875-1958), at its base decorative bronze doors by English sculptor Mr. Walter Gilbert (1871–1946) and his son Mr. Donald Gilbert (1900-1961) (Walter's daughter Margot was also an artist on the ship who created lively artwork for the Tourist Class Lounge.)

(Above) 'Merrie England' painting by Mr. Philip Connard.

On the double doors were figures from ancient legends regarding famous voyages and incidents which took place on the Sea, such as Castor and Pollux the guardians of sailors.

(Above) 'Birds of the Old World' by Mr. A. D. Carse.

(Above) 'Birds of the New World' by Mr. A. D. Carse.

Additional artwork was displayed in the dining room such as the two charming paintings of American and British birds by Mr. Andreas Duncan Carse (1876-1938) an English artist who illustrated Hans Andersen's Fairy Tales (1912). These panels perfectly embellish the space on what where hidden ventilator shafts passing vertically through the dining room from the After Turbo-Generator room below, extending up to the Top of Houses (Bridge level).

(Right) Engraved glass panels showing the story of Jason and the Golden Fleece.

There are also fourteen wood carvings that illustrate the history of shipbuilding through the ages by Mr. Edward Bainbridge Copnall (1903-1973).

Private dining rooms were located in each corner of the dining room, the two forward rooms had sliding doors that could be opened into the main dining room. In the port-side private room was artwork entitled 'The Mills Circus' by English artist Dame Laura Knight (1877-1970) while in the starboard room 'Still Life' by Mr. Herbert Davis Richter (1874-1955). The starboard room was later changed into a cocktail bar.

The two after private rooms also had artwork, in the port-side room artwork of a garden scene ('Garden') by Mrs. Vanessa Bell (1879-1961) and in the starboard side room a floral piece by Mrs. Agnes Pinder Davis .

A renown Sunday Champagne Brunch is now held in the Cabin Class Dining Room (Grand Salon) each week, it's a popular and worthwhile experience where you can savor the wide variety of sumptuous foods on offer!

Conversion Notes: The room was renamed as the 'Grand Salon.' The remaining three private dining rooms were removed. The painting 'The Mills Circus' is now displayed in the modern day coffee shop on the Promenade Deck, while the other art pieces from the private dining rooms were lost. Partitioning walls that had divided the outer sections of the room into six bays were removed, creating a more open space than original. The unused funnel shaft on C Deck (now R Deck) was converted into usable space and became the 'Windsor Room.' The additional Windsor Room space can also be combined with the Dining Room by opening folding doors. The Dining Room's floor is now mostly carpeted. The staircase behind the bronze doors was removed, and the area that they led to on B Deck now contains vending machines.

Verandah Grill

The Verandah Grill was 29 ft. long by 68 ft. wide. It was located at the after end of the Sun Deck and boasted a very distinctive semi-circular design with large windows that provided views of the open games space and ocean behind. Originally the Verandah Grill looked much different as the upper engineers quarters weren't added until after the first season when the ship was in dry dock.

(Above) After end of the Verandah Grill.

The Grill provided à la carte meals and was an alternative to the large Dining Room. It sat eighty cabin class passengers who had to pay extra to dine here. The room was also used for dancing and had a small dance floor with lights that changed color. In the evenings the Grill was used as a nightclub called the Starlight Club. The dance floor was surrounded by raised platforms that had Wilton black carpet! A cocktail bar was available on the starboard side of the room.

(Above) Striking decor inside the Verandah Grill.

Captivating murals entitled 'Entertainment' by Miss Doris Clare Zinkeisen (1898-1991) added bright colors and created a fun light atmosphere with art that depicted pantomime, theatre and the circus. The artwork had to be completely repainted in the post-war refit as it had been damaged while the room served as an antiaircraft headquarters.

Appearing like an angled column, the bottom of the aft mast penetrates the middle of the Grille on the fore end.

Conversion Notes: The two outer rooms forward of the Verandah Grill on both sides (transmitting room and Verandah Grill kitchen) were incorporated to become wings off the Verandah Grill. The room was converted to a fast food eatery in 1970, however, it was restored to it's original art deco style and rededicated on May 17th, 1997.

Tourist Class Dining Saloon

The Tourist Class Dining Saloon was located on C Deck (now R Deck) adjacent to the Tourist Class Entrance. The room was 78 ft. long and spanned the width of the deck (approximately 112 ft.) It had a capacity of four hundred guests.

A wave design was sand-blasted onto the inner windows and illuminated from behind at night. Eight decorative glazed panels at the ends of the room were also illuminated and had a cereal and fruit design.

Conversion Notes: The saloon was initially used for cold storage for the adjacent main kitchen. In the mid-1980's the wood paneling was partially dismantled and the saloon sectioned to provide space for soiled laundry, cold storage and a staff cafeteria.

Third Class Dining Saloon

The Third Class Dining Saloon was located on C Deck (now R Deck) adjacent to the Third Class Entrance. It was approximately 90 ft. long and spanned the width of the ship (118 ft.). The room seated four hundred and twelve passengers with tables set for between four and twelve diners. Two sets of double doors were on the forward wall, on either side of the main third class staircase.

(Above) Fore view of the Third Class Dining Saloon.

(Above) Front wall of the Third Class Dining Saloon. Originally the area in-front of the doors extended across between the doors on both sides of the Third Class Entrance on either sides of the ship.

Food was prepared one deck below on D Deck, in a galley that also prepared food for the crew.

Conversion Notes: The room was divided into several spaces and is mostly used for storage. The Third Class Entrance in-front of the Dining Saloon was enclosed by walls with a door on the port side, this changed the look of the broad space which used to be open across the breadth of the ship.

Lounges, Bars & Ballroom

Observation Lounge & Cocktail Bar

This semicircular lounge was located at the forward end of the Promenade Deck, at the center of the room it was 34 ft. long by 70 ft. wide. The room had twenty one large windows (5 ft. by 2 ft.) which provided passengers a wide view of the ocean.

Like the room, the cocktail bar was also semicircular, above it is a mural painting entitled 'The Royal Jubilee Week, 1935' by Mr. A. R. Thomson. Around the bar were fixed stools with a tall bright red hide top on a nickel-chromium stainless-steel bottom.

Steps forward of the bar led up to a raised seating area, that cleverly masked the increasing angle of the underlying floor as it swept upwards towards the bow with the sheer of the hull.

Conversion Notes: Originally the Promenade Deck had a walk-around passage in front of the Observation lounge, however, in the conversion the lounge was expanded outwards to include this space by removing the original forward wall of the lounge.

Cabin Class Main Lounge

The Main Lounge was located on the Promenade Deck, it was 70 ft. wide by 96 ft long and was fitted with a parquet dance floor, stage and cinema projection room and could therefore be used for a variety of purposes. The ceiling was tiered extended in height to nearly 30 ft., through both the Sun Deck and Sports Deck above.

(Above) Stage after end of the Cabin Class Main Lounge.

To entertain passengers the stage was used by celebrities and an orchestra, and on it was a concert grand piano. Above the stage gilt artwork by Mr. Maurice Lambert. On the rooms fore end was a fireplace behind which was projection equipment, accessed by a spiral staircase.

(Above) Marble fireplace on the fore end of lounge with artwork entitled 'Unicorns in Battle' by Mr. Alfred J. Oakley & Mr. Gilbert Bayes. The five square panels visible towards the middle of the artwork opened to project movies from the room behind.

(Above) View from the starboard side of the Main Lounge that clearly illustrates the ship's beautiful wood decor

Five panels above the main fireplace opened when screening movies and the room seated over four hundred Cabin Class passengers for each showing.

(Above) Vast musical themed artwork in gilt over the stage by Mr. Maurice Lambert.

Two other fireplaces were on the outer sides of the room with enormous tinted mirrors above. The impressive fireplaces were electric and had large mantels made in gold and onyx.

The room had thirty two large windows lining the Promenade Deck sides, 13 ft. in height and 2 ft. 6 in. wide.

Games were also played in the lounge, including a horse racing game which consisted of several horse cutouts moving along a track based on the number rolled with dice. Passengers also played bingo and had film quizzes were they guessed movie titles and tune names based on music played by the orchestra.

When not used for dancing the parquet floor was protected by Wilton carpet and rugs which had a green and gray leaf design.

Conversion Notes: Doors were added on the port-side for access from the Promenade Deck. The room was renamed and is now known as the Queen's Salon.

Long Gallery

The Long Gallery was an informal lounge located on the port-side of the Promenade Deck, it was appropriately named being 118 ft. long by 20 ft. wide. Passengers could enter the gallery on either the fore or after ends. It also served as an ante-room to the adjacent ballroom with two sets of doors that led into it. Etched glass panels on both outer and inner walls of the gallery provided natural light to the ballroom. On the fore end of the room was mounted a large painting entitled 'Sussex Landscape' by Mr. Bertram Nicholls (1883-1974) while on the opposite end a painting 'Evening on the Avon' by Mr. Algernon Newton (1880-1968).

After the war the gallery was extended out onto the Promenade Deck and a bar was added called 'Midships Bar and Lounge.' At this time part of the ballroom was also merged onto the Long Gallery and used as a dance floor.

Conversion Notes: The gallery was divided into several spaces accessed from doors added to the Promenade Deck, this created the Board Room, Regent Room and what is now a coffee shop. An entrance through the original gallery was also added leading to a restaurant and bar on the starboard side of the ship (Chelsea Chowder House & Bar) as well as the new rooms. The galleries paintings are in their original place but fall into the Regent Room and coffee shop. The Midships Bar was removed.

Starboard Gallery

The Starboard Gallery was located as the name indicates on the starboard side of the Promenade Deck, it was 56 ft. long by 20 ft. wide. The gallery was adjacent to the ballroom and served as an informal smoke room and lounge.

Floral paintings by Mr Cedric Morris (1889-1982) hung over the galleries fireplaces, further decoration was provided by three mural carvings by John Skeaping, including of a group of Deer in gilt and silvered mahogany. There were also decorative clocks above the rooms forward and after doors.

With changing passengers needs, in a post-war refit the gallery was combined with a portion of the ballroom and was used as a dedicated cinema. One of the Cedric Morris paintings was moved to the *RMS Queen Elizabeth*, sister ship to the *Queen Mary*.

Conversion Notes: The original Starboard Gallery space is now used as kitchens for event space and restaurants added in Long Beach, such as the Chelsea Chowder House & Bar.

(Above) One of three graceful murals that once adorned the Starboard Gallery by Mr. John Skeating.

Cabin Class Smoking Room

The Cabin Class Smoking Room was a relaxing room on the Promenade Deck and was 42 ft. wide by 69 ft. long. The room had a real coal burning fireplace, leather seats and prodigious paintings by Mr. Edward Wadsworth (1889-1949) that created captivating centerpieces to both the fore (above the fireplace) and after ends of the room.

(Above) Paintings 'The Sea' and 'Dressed Overall at the Quay' by Mr. Edward Wadsworth.

The paintings were so big they had to be brought into the Smoking Room before the doors were installed, this resulted in Wadsworth finishing the paintings on the ship, during winter and construction in Scotland.

A depiction of the *Queen Mary* was found in the background of both paintings, and showed her sailing in opposite directions in each.

Carved wooden screens by Mr. James Woodford (1893–1976) provided interest on both sides of the fireplace.

Conversion Notes: The room was renamed as the Royal Salon and doors added to the port-side Promenade Deck.

Ballroom

A ballroom was located on the Promenade Deck next to the Long Gallery. The room was 35 ft. long by 50 ft. wide and could be accessed from the Long Gallery, Starboard Gallery as well as doors on the starboard side. On the port-side of the room was a stage with a piano, and opposite a raised platform for 'tea and refreshments.'

The stage was illuminated with natural light due to an etched glass panel back-wall enabling light to shine in through the adjacent Long Gallery. Joyful murals on canvas by Miss Anna Zinkeisen (1901-1976) added decoration to the room (Anna's sister Doris Zinkeisen painted the Verandah Grill.)

After the war the ballroom was repurposed, the starboard portion of the room was merged with the Starboard Gallery to become a new dedicated cinema. The remaining section of the ballroom where the glass panels once illuminated the stage was removed creating an open area that was merged with the Long Gallery and used as a dance floor. The area between the merged Long Gallery and Ballroom was given an exquisite wood relief entitled 'Hunters Through the Ages.' In the 1950's the smaller dance floor was replaced with a boutique.

Conversion Notes: The dance floor that once was alive with music and dancing, is now the entrance to the Chelsea Chowder House & Bar.

Tourist Class Main Lounge

The Tourist Class Main Lounge was located at the after end of the Main Deck, its doors adjacent to the Tourist Class Entrance and staircase, aft of the Library and Writing Room. The lounge was 80 ft. long by 70 ft. wide and normally seated two hundred and ten passengers. It was used for dancing and also as a cinema, which increased its capacity to three hundred and eighty eight passengers.

(Above) Artwork in the Tourist Class Main Lounge.

The lounge was decorated with bright, colorful paintings on die, 'Dancing through the Ages,' by Miss Margot Gilbert, who also designed the lounges etched mirror in green glass. Years later the lounge was redecorated with a Spanish theme and called the Flamenco Room.

(Above) Playful paintings by Miss Margot Gilbert, daughter of Mr. Walter Gilbert who designed the decorative bronze doors in the Cabin Class Dining Room.

In the middle of the lounge was a dance floor, above it the ceiling rises 16 ft. in height expanding into an enclosure on the Promenade Deck, at the after end was a stage. The roof of the ceiling was used for deck games!

Conversion Notes: The lounge was restored in the original style and Miss Margot Gilbert's art once again revealed. The lounge is now known as the Britannia room.

Tourist Class Smoke Room

The Tourist Class Smoke Room was located at the after end of the Promenade Deck, it was 42 ft. long by 70 ft. wide and seated one hundred and six passengers. The room was entered from the Tourist Class Entrance hall on the fore side of the room, adjacent to the staircase.

(Above) Tourist Class Smoke Room, on the right can be seen the somber painting 'The Mauretania Arriving at Rosyth" by Mr. Charles Pears.

The room had a fireplace, six settees and tables and chairs. On one of the walls was a somber painting 'The Mauretania Arriving at Rosyth' by Mr. Charles Pears

(1873–1958) which depicted a weary RMS Mauretania billowing black smoke from her funnels with the Forth Bridge visible behind, being guided by tugs to her fate at the breakers in Rosyth, Scotland. On the forward wall of the room there was also a decorative map by Miss Herry Perry (1897-1962).

(Above) Smoke Room, now used as a Wedding Chapel.

Conversion Notes: The room is now used as a Wedding Chapel. Doors were added to the port-side from the Promenade Deck, and rooms added on the forward end.

Tourist Class Cocktail Bar

The Tourist Class Cocktail Bar was a small bar located forward of the Tourist Class Entrance on the Main Deck, adjacent to the Library and Writing Room.

Conversion Notes: The Tourist Class Cocktail Bar was removed and is now an open space.

Tourist Class Overflow Lounge

The Tourist Class Overflow Lounge was located at the after end of A Deck one deck below the larger Tourist Class Main Lounge, it was 56 ft. long by 52 ft. wide and seated around one hundred passengers.

In the middle of the room was a parquet dance floor, it was 25 ft long by 20 ft. wide and was covered with a rug when not in use. On the after end of the room was a sprayed nickel bas-relief panel by Rebel Stanton, depicting a beach scene and with a woman reaching up as if to catch a beach ball, which in the panel was actually a clock.

In the 1950's the room was renamed as the Beachcomber Club appealing to younger passengers with the inclusion of a bowling alley on the starboard side.

Conversion Notes: The room was expanded on both sides to include the outer wings that held capstan equipment. The room was renamed as the Capstan Room.

Third Class Garden Lounge

The semi-circular Garden Lounge was located towards the front of the Main Deck and measured 80 ft. wide by 35 ft. long, it was the main lounge for third class passengers and offered excellent forward views of the ocean through several portholes. The room's floor had a striking design made from Korkoid tiles.

(Above) Garden Lounge, the marquetry panel can be seen in-between the pillars on the right.

(Above) Marquetry panel entitled 'Garden Scene.'

The room had several tables with green wicker chairs (with cushions) and on the front end was a skillfully created marquetry panel entitled 'Garden Scene.' Opposite the marquetry panel on the aft end of the room was a store with large display windows.

Conversion Notes: The room was carpeted and the store was removed. The furniture is no longer in the room.

Third Class Smoke Room

The Third Class Smoke Room was a semi-circular room located on A Deck, one deck below the Garden Lounge, it was 80 ft. wide by 60 ft. There were tables and chairs for passengers, as well as armchairs and settees set in five recesses. On the port-side there was a marquetry panel depicting a hunting scene by Mr. Charles Cameron Baillie.

(Above) Third Class Smoke Room, now exhibit space.

Conversion Notes: The room is used for exhibition space and has been split into several sections. The marquetry panel was relocated on A Deck. Doors were added on the forward sides providing access outside towards the bow.

Third Class Lounge

The Third Class Lounge was located on the starboard side of B Deck and adjacent to the third class staircase. It was 60 ft. long by 30 ft. wide. In it were several tables and comfortable armchairs. On the inside wall were bookcases which could be secured with roller shutters when needed, while on the forward wall were large mirrors.

(Above) Aft view of the Third Class Lounge on B Deck.

Conversion Notes: The Third Class Lounge is now known as the Carpathia Room.

Garden Lounges

In the post-war refit additional lounges were added on the Promenade Deck, on both sides of the Tourist Class Smoke Room. The lounges were located on what was deck space, the port-side lounge was for first class passengers (renamed from cabin) and the starboard side was for second class passengers (renamed from tourist).

Conversion Notes: The port-side Garden Lounge was removed enabling visitors to walk along the entire port-side of the Promenade Deck. The starboard Garden Lounge space was incorporated into a new restaurant and several other rooms.

Mermaid Cocktail Bar

A Cocktail Bar for second class passengers (renamed from tourist) was also added in the post-war refit, on the fore end of the starboard Garden Lounge, (which was also added during the refit.) This bar replaced the Tourist Class Cocktail Bar that was located on the Main Deck, enabling the Tourist Class Playroom to be expanded.

Conversion Notes: The Mermaid Bar was removed and the space incorporated into a new restaurant.

Barber & Beauty Parlors

Gents and Ladies Hairdressers

The cabin class Gents Hairdresser and Ladies Hairdressing Shop were located amidships at the top of the staircase on B Deck. The Gents Hairdresser was aft of the Ladies Hairdressing Shop.

(Above) Originally a Gents Hairdresser on B Deck. The doors were previously on both sides of the room.

Tourist class Gents and Ladies Hairdressers were located off the Tourist Class Entrance, towards the aft end of B Deck (shown next page).

Third class passengers had a smaller Barber Shop and Beauty Parlor on A Deck adjacent to the Third Class Entrance.

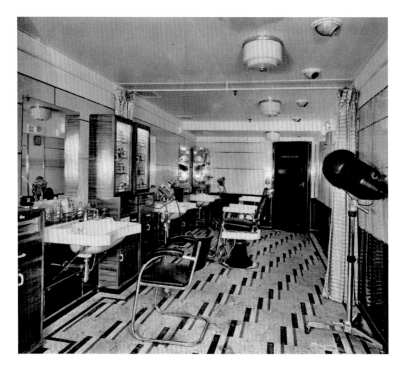

(Above) Tourist class Gents and Ladies Hairdressers, B Deck.

Conversion Notes: The cabin class Gents and Ladies Hairdressers is now an office, its doors repositioned. The tourist and third class facilities were removed.

Entertainment & Exercise

Deck Games

One hundred and twelve thousand square feet of deck space was used for deck games.

(Above) Originally three deck tennis courts were located in this space, aft of the forward funnel on the Sports Deck.

Originally there were four deck tennis courts, three on the Sports Deck behind the forward funnel and one on the Sun Deck aft of the Verandah Grill on the roof of the Tourist Lounge dome. In deck tennis a ring made of rope was used instead of a ball, the objective being to throw the ring over the net, scoring points if it lands in the opponents side. Players would try to catch the ring and throw it back over the net before it lands on their side! The scoring system was the same as regular tennis.

(Above) Passengers enjoying a blindfolded race.

Another game played on the *Queen Mary* was quoits. In quoits each player would throw several rings (made from rope) towards a jack, which was marked on the deck.

Shuffleboard was also another popular deck game were players used long sticks ('cues') to push discs into a marked out scoring zone, with different points in each area.

Conversion Notes: Wire netting used to wrap around deck game spaces and is no longer present.

(Above) Game space on the starboard side of the Sports Deck. The circular windows on the left are from the upper tier of the Cabin Class Main Lounge.

Cabin Class Gymnasium

The original Cabin Class Gymnasium was located on the port-side of the Sun Deck and measured 36 ft. long by 20 ft. wide. Its walls comprised of seven different types of wood (American walnut, Australian walnut, French walnut, teak, Australian oak, British oak and ash) and the floor had a checker-board design made of black and white marbleized squares of Korkoid.

Equipment in the Cabin Class Gymnasium:

Horse Riding Machine	2
Rowing Machine (Hydraulic)	2
Vibrating Chair	2
Belt Vibrator	2
Nautical Wheel	1
Double-Cycle Machine	1
Four Hammer Percussion Machine	1
Three Hammer Percussion Machine	1
Pulley Weight Machine	1
Punch Ball and Drum	1

An eighteen inch frieze wrapped around the inside of the gymnasiums walls with caricatures of well known sporting characters, drawn by the British cartoonist Mr. Tom Webster (1886-1962).

After a few years the gymnasium was relocated to the Sun Deck and replaced the Squash Racket Court.

(Above) Cabin Class Gymnasium.

Conversion Notes: The gymnasium was removed and the space is now used for exhibition space and a store. Some of the original gymnasium equipment is on display in the new gymnasium which is located in what was part of the No. 2 funnel shaft.

Tourist Class Gymnasium

The Tourist Class Gymnasium was located on the starboard side of the pool on F deck (now E deck). Its dimensions were 39 ft. long by 20 ft. wide, making it longer (by 3 ft. in length) than the Cabin Class Gymnasium on the Sun deck.

(Above) Looking aft in the Tourist Class Gymnasium.

Equipment in the Tourist Class Gymnasium:

Rowing Machine (Hydraulic)	2
Belt Vibrating Machine	2
Horse Riding Machine	2
Wall Bars	2
Four Hammer Percussion Machine	1
Double-Cycle Racing Machine	1
Punch Ball and Drum	1
Camel Riding Machine	1
Vibrating Chair	1
Pulley Weight Machine	1

Conversion Notes: The Tourist Class gymnasium was removed and the space is now used for exhibition space.

Squash Racket Court

The Squash Racket Court was accessed on the Sun Deck and had a viewing balcony on the Sports Deck above.

(Above) Upper level of the Squash Court, the skylight originally cast light onto a diffused glass panel ceiling.

Hours Available:

7.00 am to 1.00 pm   2.00 pm to 7.30 pm

Conversion Notes: After a few years at sea the court was replaced with the relocated Cabin Class Gymnasium. The balcony level is now used as exhibition space.

Swimming Pools

Cabin Class Swimming Pool

The Cabin Class Swimming Pool was accessed on C Deck (now R Deck) through revolving doors that led onto a balcony that overlooked the pool.

(Above) Impressive entrance to the Cabin Class Swimming Pool.

Inside the entrance and to the left were Turkish Baths, made up of several rooms; a Frigidarium (cold room), Tepidarium (warm room), Calidarium (hot room) and Laconicum (hottest room), as well as a Steam Room, Massage Room (from qualified masseuse) and Electric Baths.

The pool itself measured 35 ft. long by 22 ft. wide and was 6 ft. deep at the fore end and 4 ft. 6 in. at the after end. It held 110 tons of heated sea water, which was drained in bad weather.

(Above) Spectacular Cabin Class Swimming Pool.

The diving boards initially fitted were reportedly removed for safety as the water depth varied as the ship pitched and rolled at sea.

Charges were as follow;

Electric bath including alcohol rub	10/-
Turkish bath including alcohol rub	10/-
Inclusive charge for electric or Turkish bath including alcohol rub for the voyage	25/-
General massage	7/6
Local massage	7/6
Ultra violet irradiation	5/-
Infra-red irradiation	5/-
Ultra violet and infra-red	7/6
Diathermy	10/-
X-ray photograph and examination	1 pound

Hours available:

7:00 a.m. to 10:00 a.m.	Gentlemen
10:00 a.m. to 2:30 p.m.	Ladies
2:30 p.m. to 7:30 p.m.	Gentlemen

Conversion Notes: The Cabin Class Pool is no longer filled with water, however, can be viewed on some tours.

Tourist Class Swimming Pool

The Tourist Class Swimming Pool was located at the aft end of F Deck (now E Deck). The room measured 33 ft. by 21 ft. and the pool itself was 47 ft. long by 40 ft. wide with a depth of 6 ft. 6 in. at one end tapering to 4 ft. 6 in. on the other. The pool was lined with ivory glazed fireclay tiling, with intersecting blue bands also made from glazed fireclay.

(Above) Inside of the Tourist Class Swimming Pool.

On the port-side of the pool were ten dressing boxes for men and twelve for ladies, each set had a cold shower.

Three decoratively etched glass panels depicting underwater marine life designs by Mr. C. Cameron Baillie were mounted on the forward wall.

Conversion Notes: The Tourist Class Swimming Pool and dressing rooms were removed and became exhibition space and visitor restrooms.

Promenade Deck

Cabin Class passengers were able take a stroll or run around the entire Promenade Deck which was enclosed from the elements by windows. A lap of the Promenade Deck was 1,736 ft. It was recorded that the British Olympic runner Lord Burghley (1905-1981) ran a circuit of the Promenade Deck during the maiden voyage in under a minute, in evening dress!

(Above) Photograph of the Promenade Deck.

The deck wrapped around the front of the Observation Lounge and Cocktail Bar while a passageway aft of the Cabin Class Smoke Room also linked both sides of the Promenade Deck enabling passengers to transition from the port and starboard sides and continue their walk around the deck unobstructed. Passengers could also pass time on the Promenade Deck playing table tennis or simply lounging on a deck chair with a cup of tea or coffee.

Cost to hire deck chairs, cushions and rugs:

Deck Chairs	10/-
Cushion	5/-
Rug	5/-

The Tourist Class passengers also had a smaller promenade to walk around towards the aft end of the Main Deck.

Conversion Notes: The deck in-front of the Observation Lounge was incorporated into the lounge. With spectacular views of Long Beach, a large portion of the starboard side of the Promenade Deck was converted into restaurants. The passageway used by Tourist Class passengers to pass between the port and starboard sides of the Main Deck is now storage space (doors on both sides), however, the wooden deck planks are still visible on the floor.

Cinemas

First & Second Class Cinema

A cinema for cabin and tourist class passengers (now called first and second) was added in the 1940's in the space created by combining the Starboard Gallery and part of the Ballroom on the starboard side of the Promenade Deck.

Cabin Class Main Lounge

The Cabin Class Main Lounge on the Promenade Deck was also used as a cinema and had projection equipment in a Cinema Operating Room behind the artwork above the fireplace. As a cinema the lounge seated over four hundred passengers.

Tourist Class Main Lounge

Tourist class passengers were able to watch movies in the Main Lounge at the after end of the Main Deck, it seated up to three hundred and eighty eight passengers. A Cinema Operating Box was located on the Promenade Deck in the fore end of the ceiling dome.

Third Class Cinema

The Third Class Cinema was 60 ft. long by 30 ft. wide, it was located on the port-side of B Deck, adjacent to the third class staircase. The projection screen rolled up into the ceiling and the room also had a raised platform (stage) and dressing rooms for performers. The chairs were of contemporary design and stackable.

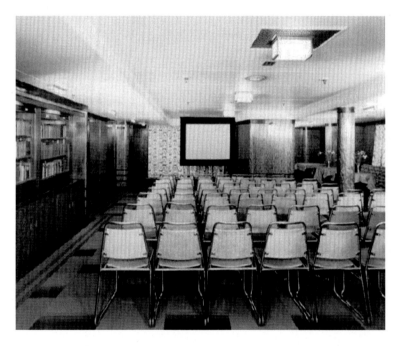

(Above) Aft view of the Third Class Cinema on B Deck, now known as the Caronia Room.

Bookcases were located on the inside wall and were secured with roller shutters.

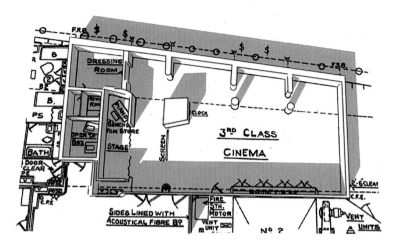

(Above) Layout of the Third Class Cinema.

Conversion Notes: The room remains as it was, however, the chairs and books are no longer present.

Playrooms

Cabin Class Playroom

The Cabin Class Playroom was located on the starboard side of the Promenade deck, aft of the Observation Lounge & Cocktail Bar. It was 40 ft. long by 18 ft. wide.

(Above) Recreated Cabin Class Playroom in original space.

A lot of attention to detail was incorporated, it had a chute for children to slide down with pirate caves underneath, a doll house, model cinema theatre to play with, and even a miniature aquarium with live tropical fish. There was also a sentry box and log cabin. Wall murals depicted teddy bears sliding down the chute and riding an old bicycle were painted by Mr. George Ramon. An ornamental sun and stars made from illuminated glass added interest to the ceiling of the room.

Tourist Class Playroom

The Tourist Class Playroom was found on the Main Deck, beside the Tourist Class Cocktail Lounge. Children played with various toys and stuffed animals that were stored in caves while above, a Royal Scot train and goods train circled the room. A toy airplane on wires appeared to fly. The walls were painted with murals themed on Noah's Ark by Miss Herry Perry (who also painted the map in the Tourist Class Smoke Room). The room was expanded in the post-war refit.

Third Class Playroom

The Third Class Playroom was located on the B Deck adjacent to the forward staircase and next to the Scroll room. Children had a variety of toys, a rocking horse and elephant and bear chairs. On the wall was a blackboard and a writing desk was also provided. The walls were illustrated with a painting about Sinbad the Sailor by Mr. C. Cameron Baillie.

Conversion Notes: Only the Cabin Class Playroom exists, inside is a mock-up of the original playroom.

Drawing Room & Writing Areas

Cabin Class Drawing Room

The Cabin Class Drawing Room is located on the Promenade Deck, on the starboard side of the Main Hall. This oval shaped room is 43 ft. long by 20 ft. wide, with six windows on the outer wall, four of them are 8 ft. tall.

(Above) Inside of the Drawing Room, now a store.

The room served as a lounge with tables and chairs, as well as a Roman Catholic chapel.

On the forward wall were hinged folding screens on which was a vibrant painting Mediterranean harbor scene by Mr. Kenneth Shoesmith. The screens could be opened to reveal an altar with sacristy and a large painting 'Madonna of the Atlantic' with gold-leaf background also by Mr. Shoesmith. A robing room was provided alongside.

On the after end of the room is a fireplace with an onyx d'or mantlepiece and a hearth made from Napoleon marble. The fireplace is surrounded by a huge painting of a flower market by Mr. Shoesmith.

(Above) 'The Flower Market' by Mr. Kenneth Shoesmith.

Conversion Notes: The room is now used as a store, the windows hidden and folding screens and altar removed.

Writing Rooms

Cabin class passengers had 32 ft. long writing areas on both sides of the Promenade Deck, forward of the doors of the Main Lounge and separated by what was the No. 2 funnel hatch in-between. The writing areas had tables and chairs for passengers to sit down and write at.

(Above) The glass panels visible above the former starboard side writing room, now a restroom.

Tourist class passengers also had a writing room that was part of the Tourist Class Library and Writing Room on the Main Deck.

Conversion Notes: The Writing Room on the port-side of the Promenade deck was converted into a store while the Writing Room on the starboard side is now a restroom. The Tourist Class Library and Writing Room is mostly storage with added walls removing all sense of what the space was used for.

Libraries

Cabin Class Library

The Cabin Class Library was located on the port-side of the promenade deck and was 44 ft. long by 20 ft. wide. It was accessed (originally only) from the Main Hall and had an attendant and a large table in the middle of the room with periodicals and magazines from both sides of the Atlantic. Over one thousand seven hundred books were available to read in bookcases separated in several alcoves, with sliding glass doors. The room had leather paneling (reducing external noise) as well as leather settees.

(Above) Alcoves that once held library books are now used to display store goods.

Conversion Notes: The library was expanded by moving the outer wall into the Promenade Deck. Doors were also added on the outer wall enabling access from the Promenade Deck. The library became a store and the bookcases are used to display store goods.

Tourist Class Library & Writing Room

The Tourist Class Library and Writing Room was a combined space for tourist class passengers and was located towards the aft end of the Main Deck.

The library area was 20 ft. long by 10 ft. wide and was decorated with two octagonal paintings by Mr. Kenneth Shoesmith, 'Richard Hakluyt Recording the Voyages of the Elizabethan Sailors' and 'Samuel Pepys at the Royal Dockyard, Deptford.' The library contained about one thousand four hundred books displayed on bookcases.

(Above) Remaining wall from tourist class library showing an octagonal frame that once held a painting by Kenneth Shoesmith. The Library and Writing Room originally extended to the right beyond the painting where a door is now located.

Extending inboard from the forward portion of the library was a writing room area, with tables for passengers to write on. On the far right wall of the Writing Room were sliding doors that could be opened to reveal an altar and another piece of art by Mr. Kenneth Shoesmith entitled 'Our Lady of the Seas.'

Conversion Notes: Both octagonal paintings have been relocated to the Board Room (Long Gallery), Promenade Deck. Only the inner wall of the library remains visible and the writing room area was divided by walls and is now mostly used for storage 'Our Lady of the Seas' was moved and displayed elsewhere on the ship.

Third Class 'Library'

Third class could read from a selection of books found in the Third Class Cinema and Third Class Lounge on the fore end of B Deck. While not primarily a library books were available on shelves on the inner walls, which could be secured using roller shutters.

Music Room

A Music Room (with grand piano) was provided on the port-side of the Promenade Deck, aft of the Observation Lounge & Cocktail Bar. Inlaid on the floor was a large clef sign motif with note symbols on both sides. Passengers used the room for practice or entertainment.

(Above) Music room recreated in the original space.

Lecture Room

Cabin class passengers could make use of the Lecture Room to share thoughts and material with a number of other passengers. The room is positioned on the Promenade Deck, aft of the Music Room and accessed from the port-side corridor which leads from the Main Hall to the Observation Lounge & Cocktail Bar. It provided a podium for the speaker and offered a slide and film projector, with seating for around thirty seven guests.

Conversion Notes: The Lecture Room now shows video footage of the Queen Mary with seats for guests and visitors to watch from.

Religious Worship

Passengers of different faiths were able to worship onboard the ship.

Aft of the third class staircase on B Deck was a Synagogue (Scroll Room) for Jewish passengers (the ship also had a Kosher kitchen), it had an electrically powered Perpetual Light that was always illuminated.

Roman Catholic services were held in the Drawing Room, on the starboard side of the Main Hall on the Promenade Deck. In this room was an altar with sacristy and large painting 'Madonna of the Atlantic' by Mr. Kenneth Shoesmith, who also painted a harbor scene on doors that screened the altar when not in use. To the right of the altar was a robing room.

On the after end of the Main Deck in the Tourist Class Library and Writing Room was an illuminated altar with a Mr. Shoesmith painting 'Our Lady of the Seas' which was covered with sliding doors when not in use.

Interdenominational services carried by the Captain were also held on Sundays in the Cabin Class Main Lounge.

Conversion Notes: The Synagogue was removed and the space used for storage. The altar and screen doors in the Drawing Room were removed, the space is now part of a store. The Tourist Class Library and Writing Room was divided by walls and is now mostly used for storage.

Passenger Communications

Passengers could phone for service, other guests, or literally anywhere in the world from the comfort of their stateroom or the phone booths.

A telephone switchboard was located on B Deck, it had five hundred and eighty five shipboard lines and ten shorelines and was staffed by up to three operators. To aid operators the board was color-coded by steward sections, with steward pantry phones on the end of each row.

(Above) Telephone booth to the left side of a display case in the Main Hall, on the Promenade Deck. In the middle a Jardiniere used to display flowers.

An aerial system used fifty two wavelengths for long distance 'ship to shore' calls, which enabling communication throughout the voyage.

(Above) Telephone exchange.

*Conversion Notes: The telephone exchange (switchboard)
was moved and is on display in the former Squash Court's
upper level. The exchange room became a hotel support
area.*

Passenger Services

Banks

A Midland bank was located on the A Deck, beside the Cabin Class Entrance. An additional bank was located beside the Tourist Class Entrance on C Deck (now R Deck).

(Above) Former bank now a gift store.

There were also three hundred and fifty small safe deposit boxes behind the pursers desk on A Deck that passengers could rent for the voyage. Each box has a lock and key. The boxes were also protected by a steel grille.

Conversion Notes: The bank on A Deck is now used as a store. The bank on C Deck was removed.

Travel Bureaus

Passengers could make travel arrangements and reserve tickets for transportation and hotels in the Travel Bureau located on the Main Deck as well as beside the Tourist Class entrance on C Deck (now R Deck).

(Above) Remaining Travel Bureau, on the Main Deck.

The travel bureaus were staffed and operated by British and Irish Railways and the Travel and Industrial Association of Great Britain and Ireland.

Conversion Notes: Only the Travel Bureau on the Main Deck remains.

Medical Facilities

Doctor's Consulting Room (A Deck)

A Doctor's Consulting Room with a two seat waiting room was located on the starboard side of A Deck beside the Cabin Class Entrance.

Conversion Notes: The Consulting Room on A Deck was removed and is now an open lounge area beside the hotel's main entrance.

Doctor's Consulting Room (B Deck)

Another Doctor's Consulting Room with exam couch and an adjacent room containing a cot and bathroom was located beside the Tourist Class Entrance on B Deck.

Conversion Notes: The Consulting Room on B Deck was converted into a guest room (B480) (the adjacent portion of the Tourist Class Entrance also became a guest room (B482)).

Hospital, Operating Theatre & Wards

The *Queen Mary* had a hospital which occupied a sizable area on the port-side of D Deck. Male and female wards were separated by a dispensary and contained multiple beds. The hospital had two bathrooms.

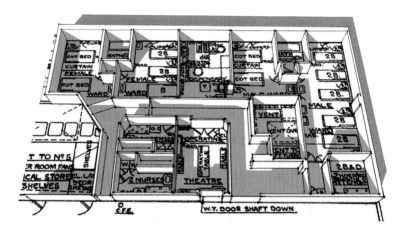

(Above) Layout of the hospital originally on D Deck.

An operating theatre was also located in the hospital and contained a Thackray operating table and ligature tables. There was a surgeon's basin and a shadowless light. A surgeon could operate at sea if necessary providing life saving care.

Conversion Notes: The hospital on D Deck was removed for exhibition space. Entrance doors were added to the side of the ship where part of the hospital had been and became the museum's main entrance.

101

Infectious Hospital (Isolation Wards)

The Infectious Hospital (perhaps better known as Isolation Wards) was located at the after end of B Deck. It was intended to isolate passengers or crew with a communicable disease from others. Separate male and female wards could each accommodate five patients, each ward had two bunk beds and a single bed. In addition to the wards were two rooms for staff as well as two bathrooms.

(Above) Restored female Isolation Ward.

Conversion Notes: The Isolation Wards were restored and reopened to visitors in 1999.

Kennels

Dogs also travelled on the *Queen Mary*, however, they were not allowed in their owners cabins and instead stayed in kennels on the port-side of the Sports Deck, accessed by a staircase from the Sun Deck.

The kennels were 30 ft. long by 15 ft. wide and accommodated twenty six pets. They were air conditioned and contained sinks with hot and cold running water, and natural light from the overhead skylight. Outside was a fenced-in exercise area that was over 80 ft. in length and which extended up steps on to the roof of the Cabin Class Gymnasium. A wooden lamppost was provided for dogs to feel at home.

Bellboys made good tips by walking pets during each voyage and owners were able to visit too.

Conversion Notes: The deckhouse that held the kennels still exists however the kennels were removed and the space used as an electrical closet.

Lifts

There were twenty-one lifts (elevators) on the *Queen Mary*, serving eleven decks. Eleven lifts were for use of passengers; of those seven were for cabin class, three for tourist class and one for third class passengers. These lifts were operated by an attendant.

Additionally two lifts were for baggage, two for food service, two for engineers, three for stores and one smaller service lift.

(Above) Two passenger lifts (elevators) on the Main Deck.

Conversion Notes: Elevator doors in the Main Hall on the starboard side were covered over with a board showing wood veneers used on the ship.

Operating the Ship

The ship was operated by a crew of one thousand, one hundred and seventy four people, under sole command of the Captain. Over the years the *Queen Mary* was commanded by thirty one different Captains.

Senior officers reporting directly to the Captain were the Staff Captain, Purser, Principal Medical Officer, Chief Radio Officer, Chief Officer, Chief Engineer and Chief Steward. Each senior officer was in command of multiple levels of officers and staff, extending down to the Bell Boys, assistant cooks etc.

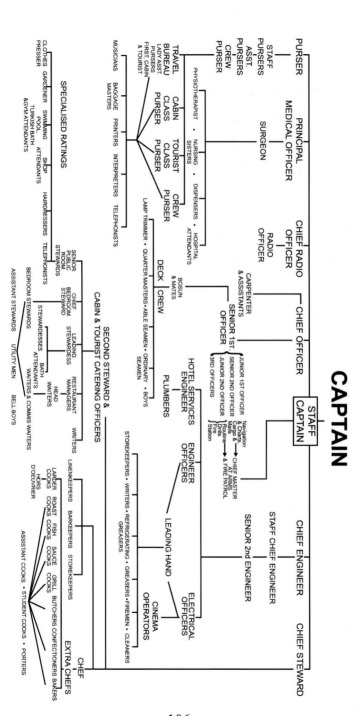

CAPTAIN

106

Ship's Officers & Identifying Rank

Commodore	One broad ring gold lace
Captain & Staff Captain	Four rings gold lace, straight
Chief Officer	Three rings gold lace, straight
Chief Engineer	Four rings gold lace, straight, with purple velvet between
Staff Chief Engineer	Four rings gold lace, straight, with purple velvet between
First Senior Second Engineer	Three rings gold lace, straight, with purple velvet between
Purser	Three rings gold lace, straight, with white velvet between
Staff Purser	Two and a half rings gold lace, straight, white velvet between
Physician & Principal Medical Officer	Three rings gold lace, straight, with red velvet between
Surgeon	Three rings gold lace, straight, with red velvet between
Chief Steward	Three rings gold lace, zig-zag
Second Steward	Two rings gold lace, zip-zag

Captains of the Queen Mary

Commodore Sir Edgar T. Britten	12/1/35
Captain George Gibbons	1/29/36
Commodore Reginald V. Peel	8/4/36
Commodore Robert B. Irving	11/11/36
Captain Ernest M. Fall	4/9/41
Commodore Sir James Bisset	2/23/42
Commodore Sir Cyril G. Illingworth	8/10/42
Captain Roland Spencer	7/29/44
Commodore Chas. M. Ford	3/11/46
Commodore George E. Cove	12/6/46
Commodore Sir C. Ivan Thompson	2/15/47
Captain John A. MacDonald	3/6/47
Captain John D. Snow	7/4/47
Commodore Harry Grattidge	12/31/48
Captain Harry Dixon	7/20/50
Captain Robert G. Thelwell	8/13/51
Captain Donald W. Sorrell	8/19/52
Commodore George G. Morris	6/27/56
Commodore Chas. S. Williams	6/25/57
Captain Alexander B. Fasting	9/11/57
Captain Andrew MacKellar	8/26/58
Commodore John W. Caunce	10/22/58
Commodore Donald M. MacLean	6/24/59

Captain James Crosbie Dawson	3/30/60
Captain Sidney A. Jones	5/25/60
Commodore Frederick G. Watts	8/9/60
Captain Eric A. Divers	6/19/62
Commodore Geoffrey T. Marr	5/7/64
Captain John Treasure Jones	9/8/65
Captain William E. Warwick	9/15/65
Captain William J. Law	5/3/67

*Date shown is of first command

Captain & Deck Officers Quarters

Quarters for the captain and deck officers were located directly below the Bridge, on the Sports Deck. A staircase behind the Bridge led down to the crew cabins and continued down to the Sun Deck where other crew cabins were also located, including those of the wireless transmitter operators.

The captain naturally had the largest quarters and had a dayroom, bedroom and private bathroom. In the dayroom he held cocktail parties and entertained elite passengers twice a day, except during bad weather.

(Above) Captain's bedroom. His dayroom was through the door on the left, where he entertained guests.

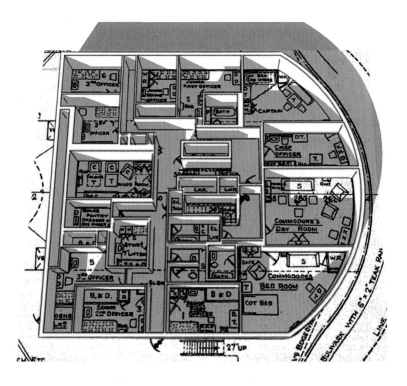

(Above) Layout of the captain and deck officers quarters on the Sports Deck.

There was a stewards cabin and pantry, and amongst the rooms there was also a Ward Room where officers met daily.

(Above) Remaining quarters on the Sports Deck. Originally this space contained several other rooms and a staircase that led up to the Bridge.

Conversion Notes: The staircase that led from the Bridge to the quarters below was removed and the floor sealed. Rooms, including the captains private bathroom were removed to permit large numbers of visitors to pass through the space. The remaining rooms display the original decor and use of the rooms, while an exhibit showcases uniforms.

Engineers' Quarters

Engineers had dedicated spaces in several areas of the ship while the officers originally had quarters on the Sun Deck which included a ward room and cabins. Additional rooms were added when the ship was in dry dock (late 1936 - early 1937) by adding to the roof of the Verandah Grill. Elevators went from these quarters directly down to the engine rooms. Much later a ward room was added in what was the Cabin Class gymnasium.

The engineers dining room was on D Deck and could seat fifty eight engineers at a time.

(Above) Engineers quarters on top of the Verandah Grill.

(Above) Engineers dining room.

Conversion Notes: Engineers quarters on the Sports Deck were converted into a restaurant, now called Sir Winston's, the windows were extended in the style of the Verandah Grill below. The quarters on the Sun Deck are now used as administrative offices.

Stewards & Stewardesses

Over three hundred stewards and stewardesses looked after the needs of passengers during a voyage. Passengers had colored buttons in their staterooms to call for a steward or stewardess, the red buttons called for a steward, while the green buttons called for a stewardess. When pressed an indicator lamp in the hallway and in the stewards pantry illuminated (there were over two thousand five hundred lights.) Service was available twenty four hours a day.

Gardener

A ship's gardener took care of twelve thousand plants aboard the *Queen Mary*, they added bright colors throughout the ship, with flowers on the main stairway landings and placed on tables in the restaurants and lounges. The gardener had a room to work in on the portside of the Sun Deck with a sink, cold box, bench and drawers.

Crew Life on Board

Known by crew as the "working alleyway" there was a long passageway (also referred to as "Burma Road" after World War II) on the port-side of D and E Deck (now called C and D Deck) that permitted crew to move swiftly around the ship out of sight of passengers.

(Above) Part of the crew alleyways.

The crew also had their own makeshift recreational area and service bar in the space around the Stores and Baggage Entrance at the after end of C Deck (now R Deck.) This area was called the Pig and Whistle ("Pig") here crew could relax with a drink, socialize with each other, smoke a cigarette and play darts or card games.

Gambling also took place, with dart tournaments and card games such as poker, there was also bingo games and raffle drawings. Famous passengers would sometimes join the crew and provide entertainment and on occasion the crew would also put on their own shows.

Crew also had a single seat Barbers Shop on the starboard side of E Deck (now D Deck) adjacent to crew quarters.

Conversion Notes: Huge areas of the D and E Deck where the crew passageway existed were removed. The Pig and Whistle area is now a storage area. The crews Barber Shop was removed.

Wheelhouse

The Wheelhouse (Bridge) of the *Queen Mary* was the control hub of the mighty vessel, from here the captain and officers operated the entire ship with a towering view of the bow and ocean ahead.

(Above) Navigating Bridge.

On the Bridge the helmsman steered the ship using one of two wheels (there was an extra wheel incase of failure of one.) The ship could also be kept on course automatically by the gyro-pilot ("Iron Mike") whose servos were linked to the rudder hydraulic actuators, any change of heading would result in rudder movement to regain course.

Engine power and therefore the ship's speed was controlled from the Bridge using telegraphs to send commands down to the engineers deep in the engine-rooms, there was a telegraph for each of the four engines. To send a command, officers moved the lever on the telegraph to one of the desired positions which then showed in the corresponding position on the receiving telegraph. Engineers then moved the lever on their telegraph to the same position to acknowledge the instruction, before manually setting the commanded power. Another telegraph sent steering commands (during docking) to the officer on the Docking Bridge on the after end of the Promenade Deck.

Navigation was fairly rudimentary using charts in combination with a gyro compass. The course was recorded electrically from the gyro and a record was also kept of the depth of sea-bed. There was also a Chernikeef Log, this was a small propellor on the end of a 3 ft. long brass rod that was extended from the port-side of H Deck (now G Deck) into the water which drove a generator. Its output was displayed in the Bridge as speed and distance.

Other equipment on the Bridge included revolution indicators to monitor the propellor shafts rotational speeds, a sound-proof cabinet, a watertight doors indicator and buttons to sound the whistles. There were also two clocks, one showing Greenwich time, the other the time in New York.

Navigating the RMS Queen Mary

Officers plotted the ships position on charts in a chart room at the starboard after end of the Bridge, the captain had a separate chart room on the port-side.

(Above) Officer's chart room.

A wireless direction-finder and master compass were located on the Compass Platform (above the Bridge), the compass indication was relayed and displayed at other locations by four repeaters and this was used to steer the ship. The course was recorded and the last 30 days were viewable.

Communication

Telegraphs

Electric telegraphs were positioned around the ship to send and acknowledge commands for functions including steering, engines, docking, anchors and cables.

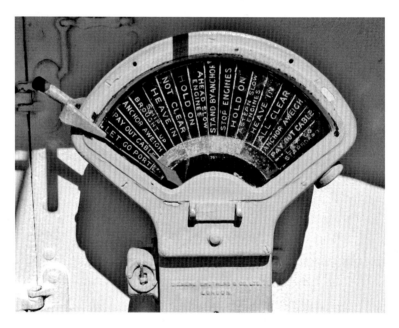

(Above) A telegraph mounted on the bow of the ship.

Changes on the Bridge telegraphs would show on applicable telegraphs such as in the engine-room, and officers acknowledged commands using their telegraph.

Loudaphone

Loudaphones were a special type of telephone used by crew, they reduced background noise and were therefore used in noisier places such as the engine room. They were used in sixty two locations around the ship, including in the Bridge, Crow's Nest and at each lifeboat station.

(Above) A Loudaphone found in the aft engine room.

Voice Pipes

Voice Pipes were simply pipes that crew spoke into transmitting their voice through the pipe to the person on the other end. Flared ends amplified the sound.

Radio Communications

The *Queen Mary* was able to communicate with both sides of the Atlantic continuously during a voyage using radio, telephone, telegraphs and even broadcast radio.

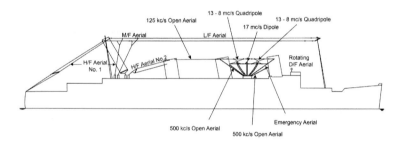

(Above) Antenna's on the *Queen Mary*.

Ten independent antennas facilitated communications using long wave, medium wave and short wave transmissions. Radio officers had a Wireless Transmitting Room and 250 ft. further forward a Wireless Receiving Room, both located on the Sun Deck.

An emergency transmitter with at least a 500 mile range was provided with a dedicated generator and twenty four Exide battery auxiliary power source.

Steering

Ship's direction was controlled by rotation of a colossal rudder at the aft end of the ship. Wash from the the propellers acted against the rudder turning the ship.

The rudder weighed 140 tons yet was hollow inside which added buoyancy. On the sides were two doors, inside was a steel ladder and platforms to permit inspection.

The rudder stock (forward part of rudder) extended up into a steering room above the waterline on the F Deck (now called E Deck). On top of the mast was a tiller turned by four cast-steel electric-hydraulic rams those cylinders were actuated by oil pressure. The steering gear was the largest built in Britain at that time, weighing 180 tons.

(Above) Hydraulic ram and steering mechanism.

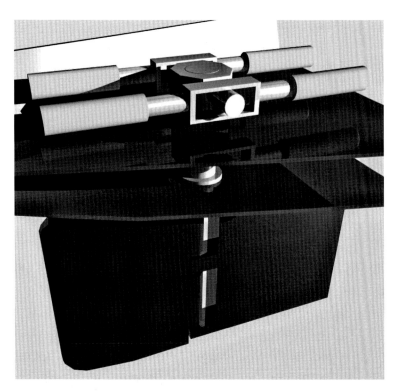

(Above) 3d render of the steering gear and rudder stock extending down to the rudder. The rams moved the crosshead which rotated the rudder stock, turning the rudder below.

Oil pressure was maintained by three 250 BHP electrically driven pumping units (one normally a reserve).

If necessary the ship could be steered with two opposing rams and only one of the pump units. The electric pumps normally on the main electric switchboard could also be powered from the emergency switchboard.

The rudder could be turned at several locations on the ship, with wheels in the navigating bridge, below the docking bridge, and also beside the hydraulic steering rams themselves.

(Above) Wheel in the steering room on what was F Deck.

Stabilizers

The *Queen Mary* rolled from side to side in heavy weather more than had been expected. Passenger corridors initially did not have hand rails and it was necessary to quickly add them as can be seen today.

Four 98 ton Denny Brown anti-rolling stabilizers were added in 1958, costing £500,000. They were extended from the Bridge in rough seas, extending 11 ft. 4 in. from the sides of the ship in less than two minutes.

(Above) Stabilizer controls in the Bridge.

Conversion Notes: The stabilizers were removed and the openings sealed.

Propulsion

In this area of the book we explore how the *Queen Mary's* 80,773 tons were propelled by her four massive propellers and we explore the mighty propulsion system that drove them.

A quick overview before delving into the details;

The first step was creating steam in the twenty four boilers:

• Air was forced into the boiler rooms to aid combustion.

• Water was softened to remove particles.

• Fuel was burned to create heat.

• Heat evaporated softened water to create steam.

The next step was using the steam:

• Steam from boilers was routed to engine rooms.

• Four steam powered turbines per engine rotated the main gear (one per engine) to which the propeller was connected via a shaft.

Fuel

Four steam powered turbines per engine rotated the propeller. To create the large volume of steam needed to drive the turbines Bunker C type oil-fuel was ignited inside boilers, the immense heat generated (700 degrees Fahrenheit) was used to evaporate softened water that circulated between steel drums in the furnace of the boilers.

The oil-fuel was stored in forty six large fuel bunkers along the sides of the ship (twenty three on each side) that extended nearly four decks high and that were 368 ft. in length. Total fuel capacity was 2,398,000 gallons (8,630 tons) yet the ship could be fueled in eight hours utilizing six filling stations that were located on D Deck. The quantity (weight) of remaining oil-fuel in the bunkers was read on Pneumercator gauges.

Oil-fuel usage:

- Atlantic crossing burned over 1,258,600 gallons
- 1,050 tons every 24 hours (43.75 tons per hour)
- thirteen feet per gallon (406 gallons per mile)
- one barrel of fuel every 12 seconds

Conversion Notes: The Oil Filling Stations on D Deck were removed.

Air

A large volume of air was needed (20,000 tons per day) for combustion of the oil-fuel. The air was supplied in a closed-stokehold system of forced draught, that meant air was provided under pressure to the boiler rooms by thirty two electrically-driven fans (eight in each main boiler-room) which drew air from large ventilators on the upper deck. As the air was being forced into the boiler rooms air pressure was higher than normal and air-tight doors were used to move between the rooms (there were thirteen air-locks between E and H Decks). The boiler rooms were air tight therefore the boiler furnaces were supplied air from the surrounding room under pressure.

Water Softening Plant

Three and a half million gallons of sea water was turned into steam each day. It was first purified in the Water Softening Plant forward of No. 1 Boiler Room which helped to reduce scale deposits and corrosion inside the metal 'water tubes' in which the water circulated inside the boilers. The Water Softening Plant could soften 300 tons of water a day and the purified water was then stored in tanks prior to being used in the boilers.

Conversion Notes: The Water Softening Plant was removed, however, the space can be seen on tours.

Boilers

Steam for propulsion was generated in twenty four Yarrow water-tube boilers located across four boiler rooms, each room contained six boilers grouped in two rows of three. They occupied a space 80 ft. by nearly 270 ft. and each boiler was approximately 31 ft. high. Twelve of the main boilers were smaller with a working water level of 14 tons, the larger ones a capacity of 17 tons (372 tons total).

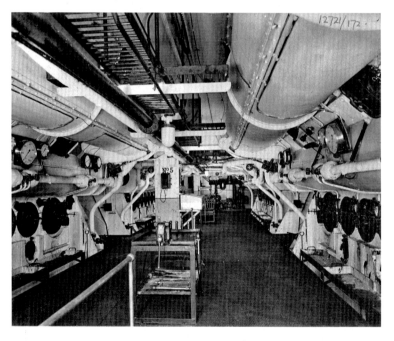

(Above) No. 5 Boiler Room.

The boilers produced high pressure steam at 425 lb. per sq. inch that was superheated to a temperature of 700 degrees Fahrenheit.

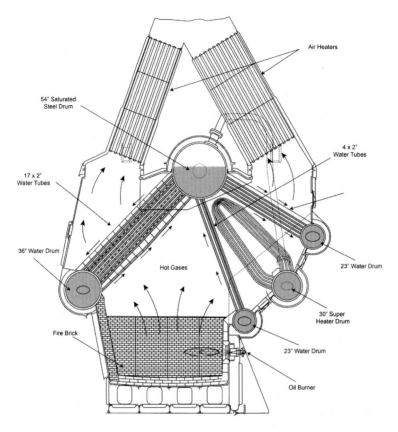

Air Heaters

54" Saturated
Steel Drum

4 x 2"
Water Tubes

17 x 2"
Water Tubes

36" Water Drum

Hot Gases

23" Water Drum

Fire Brick

30" Super
Heater Drum

23" Water Drum

Oil Burner

(Above) Illustration of a Yarrow water-tube boiler. Fuel was burned in the bottom section and the hot gases heated the water which circulated between the drums in a multitude of tubes. The hot gases then were routed up and out of the smoke stacks while the steam from the steam drum was routed to the turbines.

To create steam, the purified sea water (sea water treated in the Water Softening Plant) was heated inside the boilers by igniting oil-fuel using seven burners (per boiler) (one hundred and sixty eight burners in total for the twenty four boilers). Each boiler was lined with Firebrick retaining heat (about 500 tons of firebrick was used in the boilers).

The heat of the ignited oil-fuel in the furnace of the boiler heated the water which circulated between a steam drum (whopping 4 ft. 6 in. diameter) and four other drums, connected by a multitude of steel 'water' tubes. Over one hundred and sixty thousand water and steam tubes were in the twenty four boilers. As the water temperature increased, steam was produced (80,000 lbs. per boiler, per hour).

The twenty four boilers produced 1,920,000 lbs. of steam per hour, some 16 tons every minute.

Drums in each main water-tube boiler:

Water drums (23")	2
Water drum (36")	1
Saturated steam drum (54")	1
Super heater drum (30")	1

The warm (and sometimes smoky) air from the boilers was channeled to the smoke stacks and exhausted high above the upper decks and away from passengers.

High pressure steam coming from the boilers was routed by insulated pipes to the main engines turbines, located in two engine rooms. There was 2,600 ft. of main steam piping with an internal diameter of 16 in. for the ahead turbines and 12 1/2 in. for the astern pipes.

(Above) High pressure steam pipe.

In addition to the Yarrow boilers there were also three Scotch (auxiliary) double-ended cylindrical boilers located in No. 1 Boiler Room. The superheated steam they generated powered seven turbo-generators which created the ship's electrical power. These boilers had a diameter of 17 ft. 6in. and were 22 ft. long.

(Above) No. 3 Boiler room with boilers removed.

Conversion Notes: All of the boilers were removed and the boiler rooms are now cavernous spaces. Boiler room 1 and 2 can be seen on tours. Boiler room 5 was incorporated into the exhibition hall.

Steam Turbines

Known as 'Parsons quadruple expansion single reduction geared turbines,' the arrangement was named after Charles Parsons (who patented the first workable turbine in 1884). The system routed high pressure steam (from the boilers) through four steam-turbine engines (hence quadruple) per main engine, they each had a gear wheel (pinion) that spun rapidly due to the rotation of the turbine blades and these gear wheels meshed against a large gear in the main engine rotating it and the connected propellor shaft.

There were thousands of turbine blades in each turbine (257,000 in each set, each fitted by hand) that were spun by steam pressure using impulse-reaction forces.

The turbines were named in a way that indicated the loss of steam pressure as the steam was routed through each turbine. As a result of the loss of pressure, blades in the low pressure turbines were larger.

The four turbines (per engine) were;

- First turbine
- First intermediate pressure stage
- Second intermediate
- Fourth low pressure turbine

The engines were single-reduction geared type. This meant that as the turbine pinions rotated much quicker than desired for the propeller shaft (thousands of revolutions per minute), the rotational speed was reduced by engaging the smaller pinion wheels against the engines larger wheel. Each revolution of the smaller pinions turned the much larger gear wheel a fraction of its circumference, resulting in a slower rotation of the propeller shaft (around 200 revolutions per minute at maximum power).

The turbine blades used impulse-reaction forces, that meant that high-pressure steam was directed onto the turbine blades, pushing and rotating the blades, similar to how water rotates a waterwheel (impulse force), the steam reaction from striking the blades caused a reaction.

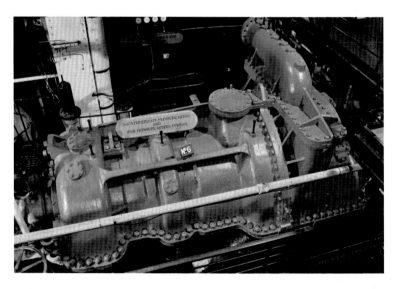

(Above) The intermediate-pressure turbine those blades were driven by steam pressure produced in the boiler rooms.

Main Engines

The *Queen Mary* had four main engines, one to turn each of her propellers. The space occupied by them was huge, approximately 150 ft. long by 110 ft. wide and 40 ft. high. There were two engine rooms, the Forward and After engine rooms, deep in the lower decks of the ship. The Forward Engine Room held two engines that rotated the outer wing tail-shafts and propellers, and in the After Engine Room were two engines that drove the inboard shafts and propellors. The main engines could collectively generate 160,000 horsepower.

To understand how the engines worked, visualize a propeller, linked by a long shaft to a large gear wheel.

(Above) Model showing propeller linked by a shaft to a large gear wheel.

These gear wheels were 14 ft. in diameter and accurate to one thousandth of an inch, they took two months to cut.

Four steam powered turbines (per engine) were grouped around each gear wheel (as shown below) with their pinions (rotating shafts) meshed against the big gear wheel. The four turbines contained thousands of blades that were rotated by steam pressure from the boiler rooms, these blades rotated the pinions and in-turn rotated the gear wheel, tail-shaft and propellers.

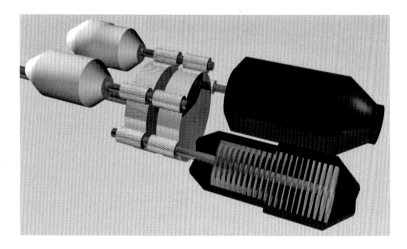

(Above) Simplified illustration showing a main gear wheel (looks like two wheels in the middle) and propeller shaft being rotated by four steam turbines. The bottom right turbine is shown open to reveal the turbine blades inside that were driven by steam pressure from the boilers.

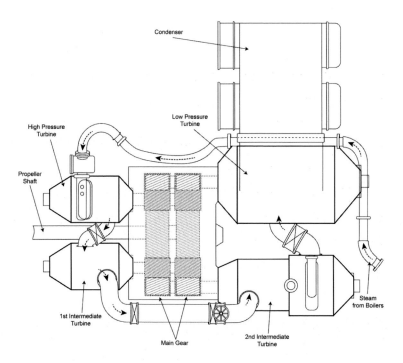

Condenser

Low Pressure
Turbine

High Pressure
Turbine

Propeller
Shaft

1st Intermediate
Turbine

Main Gear

2nd Intermediate
Turbine

Steam
from Boilers

(Above) Illustration of a main engine, comprising off four steam-turbines meshed again the gear wheel in the middle. The propeller shaft extends to the left from the gear wheel. The arrows (starting right side) indicate how the steam flowed through all four turbines before reaching the condenser.

(Above) Main gear (top) being rotated by the pinion off a steam-turbine (bottom).

Pinion Gear Statistics:

	RPM	Teeth	Diameter
Main Gear Wheel	180	443	13' 6.4942"
High Pressure	1533	52	1' 7.7098"
1st Intermediate	1533	52	1' 7.7098"
2nd Intermediate	1035	77	2' 4.8799"
Low Pressure	1035	77	2' 4.8799"

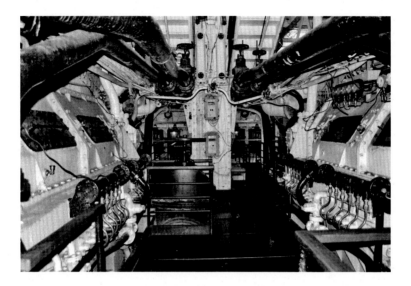

(Above) After engine room facing aft and in-between the two remaining engines that drove the inner propellers. The access panels in black cover two of the turbine's pinions where they meshed against the main gear wheels (as shown next page). In-front and behind the engines are the steam-turbines.

Conversion Notes: Only two main engines and associated machinery in the After Engine Room remain, the Forward Engine Room was removed during conversion.

Condensers

Once the steam exhausted from the turbines, it was converted back into water in gargantuan condensers (one per engine). The condensers were 28 ft. high by 20 ft. wide, and over 20 ft. long, they weighed a whopping 178.32 tons each (empty). Inside each condenser was thirteen thousand seven hundred and eighty copper-nickel alloy tubes, each 15 ft. 6 in. long and of 3/4 in. diameter (41,000 sq. ft. of cooling surface.) The condensing rate was 4 tons of steam per minute (480,000 lbs. per hour).

When the steam condensed to water, it was used again in the boilers and converted back to high-pressure steam.

Conversion Notes: As part of the Long Beach conversion all of the boiler rooms and forward engine room were removed for exhibition space.

Propeller Shafts

To rotate the propellers and propel the ship each of the propellers were connected by a long hollow tail-shaft to one of four main engines. In total there was 1,024 ft. of propeller shafting, supported by bearings.

(Above) Rusted port inboard propellor shaft which linked the propeller to a main engine.

The propeller shafts had a diameter of 28 in. and were hollow, with walls 11 to 13 inches thick. They rotated at around 200 rpm. Horsepower was measured electrically by a Torsion Meter (shown on next page). The tail-shafts passed through watertight apertures as they exited the ships hull, as naturally they were below the water surface level.

(Above) Torsion Meter which electrically measured torque and displayed it as shaft horsepower.

Large starting gears prevented distortion of the shafts by slowly rotating the shafts one revolution every 9.8 minutes. During her life at sea the propeller shafts were continuously oiled and a bare metal color, however, after decades of disuse they are now rusted and an orange rust color.

Conversion Notes: Only the two inboard propeller shafts remain, the outer shafts were removed in Long Beach to make room for exhibition space.

Propellers

The *Queen Mary* had four large propellers that were mounted under the aft end of the ship.

(Above) Men working perilously on the *Queen Mary's* starboard outer propeller, the inner propellor visible in the distance.

The propellers were also known as screws, making the *Queen Mary* a 'quadruple-screw.'

They were the heaviest ever cast, starting at 55 tons and ending up weighing 35 tons. Each measured 18 ft. from tip to tip, however, despite the size and weight the propellors were so finely balanced they could be moved by mere finger pressure. They cost £7,000 and were made from special high-tensile manganese bronze.

Throughout the *Queen Mary's* career she received twenty two sets of new propellers which were swapped out in dry-dock.

(Above) Propeller fairing cone (weighs around 1 ton) and securing nut on display on the *Queen Mary*.

(Above) One of the *Queen Mary's* propellers on display at the entrance to the cruise terminal in Long Beach, California, adjacent to the *RMS Queen Mary*. It was erected by the Queen Mary Club of the Long Beach Chamber of Commerce and dedicated on December 9th, 1973.

Conversion Notes: To be classified as a building in retirement three of the four propellers were removed. Only the port inboard propeller remains and can be seen from inside a specially constructed 60 ton box added to the side of the ship, it contains approximately 200,000 gallons of water! Visitors can enter the box from the F Deck (now E Deck) and look down to view the propellor. Of the removed propellers; a propeller is on display at the entrance to the cruise terminal in Long Beach (near the ship), a propeller is displayed on the lawn of LA Fire Department Station 112 in Los Angeles, one was melted down for souvenirs, and a spare is believed to be dockside near the ship.

Smoke Stacks

Three smoke stacks (funnels) rise high above the ship's superstructure and were used to discharge smoke and exhaust from the boiler rooms below. They were painted in an iconic red with a black band on top.

(Above) Enormous middle Smoke Stack (replacement.)

After wind tunnel tests using models, the stacks were graduated in height to ensure that smoke would not engulf the passenger deck spaces.

(Above) Funnel hatch converted in Long Beach into a gym.

Conversion: The stacks were removed in Long Beach to enable removal of machinery from the boiler rooms, they collapsed on the dockside under their own weight and were replaced with stainless steel replicas that were shorter in height. Made up of several sections and welded, the replacements have a smoother appearance to the originals which were riveted together. Since the funnel hatches were no longer required they were converted into new spaces such as the Windsor room and a gymnasium.

Electrical System

The *Queen Mary* was considered to be substantially an all-electric ship. The main electric plant consisted of seven turbo-generators, each with an output of 1,300 kW.

Around the ship 735 miles of heavy electrical cable was used (12 miles of it was 1 inch in diameter). In total 4,300 miles of wiring was used (weighing 340 tons) and powered more than 30,000 lamps.

To create electricity, steam was produced in three Scotch fire-tube boilers, these were located in the No. 1 Auxiliary Boiler Room on H Deck (now G Deck). Scotch fire-tube boilers worked differently to water-tube boilers as the heat moved through tubes which ran through the water heating it, whereas in water-tube boilers the water moves inside tubes, heated by the surrounding hot gases from the burners.

Steam from the Scotch boilers was routed to two turbo-generator rooms also on H Deck (now G Deck); the Forward Turbo Generator Room with three turbo-generators for hotel services (lighting, heating, lifts etc.) and the After Turbo Generator Room with four turbo-generators for the ship's auxiliary services (various pumps and fans). In each turbo-generator the steam powered a ten stage turbine which then drove a DC Generator via single reduction gearing. Electricity was then transmitted along ring mains and distributed to services at a multitude of switchboards.

(Above) Men installing one of the ship's turbo-generators.

Two Parsons eight-cylinder kerosene engines with 75 kw DC generators were provided for emergency use and were located on B Deck. Additionally there were batteries for low-voltage usage.

(Above) Utilities are now supplied from the adjacent pier.

Conversion Notes: Electric power is now provided from the adjacent pier and is not produced onboard. The No. 1 Auxiliary Boiler Room and both of the turbo-generator rooms were removed.

Kitchens

Cabin and Tourist Class Kitchens

The main kitchens were located on C Deck (now R Deck) ingeniously in-between and serving both the Cabin Class Dining Room and the Tourist Class Dining Room. The kitchens were 150 ft. long and spanned the entire width of the ship.

(Above) Large ovens in the kitchen.

The kitchens had a variety of equipment including electric ovens, cold pantry, salamander, potato-peeling machines, mixing machines, waffle machine and even a dough mixing machine with a 280 lb. capacity. There was also an ice cream machine with two nickel containers with a 20 lb. capacity. In the kitchens where machines for washing glasses and dishes.

Third Class and Kosher Kitchen

A smaller kitchen for third class passengers and crew, as well as an adjoined Kosher kitchen were located on the forward port-side of D Deck (now C Deck).

Conversion Notes: The main kitchen equipment was removed. A corridor was added on the port-side in-between the Cabin Class Dining Room and Tourist Class Dining Room and a new entrance cut in the hull for an entrance from the wharf-side. Both the third class and Kosher kitchens were removed.

Voyage Supplies

Poultry	4,000 chickens & ducks
Milk	4,000 gallons
Tea & Coffee	4,000 lbs.
Butter	3 tons
Cheese	2,000 lbs.
Milk	70 tons
Eggs	70,000
Fish	20 tons
Vegetables	40,000 lbs.
Potatoes	30 tons
Sugar	10,000 lbs.
Wine	10,000 bottles
Spirits	5,000 bottles
Drought Beer	6,000 gallons
Bottled Beers	40,000 bottles
Minerals	60,000 bottles
Cigars	5,000

Anchors & Chains

The *Queen Mary* had two massive 18 ft. tall, 16 ton anchors that were stowed in recesses high in the sides of the bow of the ship (to reduce wind resistance). They were attached to chains that were 990 ft. long (165 fathoms) and weighed 145 tons.

(Above) Two anchor chains that lead down to the anchors held in recesses on the sides of the ship.

The chains were tested to a strain of 700 tons, which far exceeded the required 400 tons of pressure.

(Above) Towering anchor on display on E Deck (now D Deck) in the exhibition space above the remaining (aft) engine room.

Printers

A printers shop was located forward of the ships hospital on the port-side of D Deck. A variety of items were printed onboard, including a daily newspaper entitled 'Ocean Times' as well as a 'Programme of Events,' 'Concert Programme' and passenger lists. Twelve thousand menus a day were also printed with reproduced paintings on the cover and which are considered collectible today.

Conversion Notes: The printers shop was removed.

Cargo, Mail & Baggage

The *Queen Mary* had two main cargo holds, #1 & #2, both at the front of the ship. Hold #2 was larger and could store thirty-six cars. Shafts permitted steel derricks to lower cargo down to the holds on platforms. The derricks could each lift 5 tons and vary in length from 52-72 feet.

RMS in the *Queen Mary's* name was an abbreviation for 'Royal Mail Ship' and indicated that she was under contract to deliver British Royal Mail. Electric hoists and chutes were used to load mail, which was stored in lower deck spaces in both the fore and aft sections of the ship.

(Above) View from bow looking aft towards Bridge shows the derricks that once lifted cargo platforms.

Passenger baggage was loaded using lifts (elevators) and placed in baggage holds in the lower decks, which were in sections both fore and aft. Cherbourg mail and baggage was stored to both sides of the tourist class swimming pool on G Deck (now F Deck.)

(Above) Electric cargo winch.

Conversion Notes: An elevator was fitted in Hold #2 cargo shaft during conversion. The baggage spaces on G Deck were removed and form part of exhibition space.

Safety at Sea

HOW THE QUEEN WAS SEEN & HEARD

Whistles

The *Queen Mary* had three steam whistles, two on the forward funnel and one on the middle funnel, each whistle was approximately 6 ft. 7 in. long and weighed 2,205 lb. They were mounted high on the funnels and could be accessed from platforms that towered sixty five feet above the deck below.

(Above) Two whistles mounted on the forward funnel.

The whistles were activated electrically by use of push buttons on the Bridge and Bridge wings. At least one whistle could also be controlled manually by hand from the

Bridge by utilization of a wire, this extended to a lever on the base of the whistle which when pulled caused a steam valve to open sounding the horn.

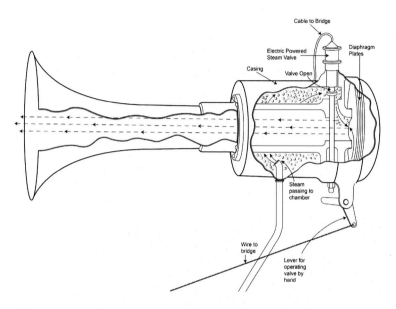

(Above) Cutaway view of a steam whistle.

The whistles were operated by 140 lb. per sq. inches of steam pressure which was fed into a circular chamber around the base of the each horn. When activated a steam valve opened which permitted the steam to pass through the valve under pressure, it then impinged four diaphragm plates (22 1/2 in. diameter) causing vibration of the plates. The vibration generated the intense tone which was keyed to lower bass A and could be heard ten miles away!

Conversion Notes: One whistle on the forward funnel still works and is regularly sounded to the delight of visitors, it now uses compressed air and not steam pressure as it originally had done. The whistle from the middle funnel was restored and fitted to the RMS Queen Mary 2.

Speakers

The *Queen Mary* was initially fitted with Marconi loud speakers on both ends of the ship, this enabled the pilot to immediately broadcast audible instructions from the Bridge to tug boats when docking the ship.

Queen Mary's Bells

The *Queen Mary* had three bells. The largest bell hung above the crow's nest, it was made from copper and tin and made an F note sound. The bell has a diameter of 24 inches and weighed 350 pounds! It could be heard half a mile away.

(Above) Largest bell that hung above the crow's nest.

The second largest bell is mounted right at the bow of the ship, it has a diameter of 18 inches and made a B note sound (shown on next page).

(Above) Second largest bell on the *Queen Mary* hangs on the bow of the ship.

Outside the Wheel House was the smallest bell with a diameter of 10 inches, it weighed 30 pounds and made a B note sound.

Conversion Notes: The largest bell that originally hung above the crow's nest is mounted outside the Main Hall on the Promenade Deck. The smallest bell was sold at auction.

Searchlights

The *Queen Mary* had two powerful searchlights positioned on the Compass Platform above the Wheelhouse and in the forward corners of the deck. This enabled illumination along the port and/or starboard sides of the ship. Wooden steps outside the Wheelhouse enabled officers to quickly go up to the Compass Platform and use the searchlights if needed.

(Above) Examples of searchlights found onboard the *Queen*.

The 'Sperry' searchlights were 18 inch diameter high intensity arc type lights, mounted on pedestals which enabled operation by hand. Inside was a 55 ampere lamp and parabolic reflecting mirror. A hinged door on the unit enabled either a wide area to be illuminated or alternatively a smaller area with a narrow beam of light.

Navigating & Other Lights

In addition to searchlights the *Queen Mary* also had colored navigating lights around the ship which assisted other ships in seeing the ship at night and in low visibility. The lights were electric, however, in an emergency oil filled lanterns could alternatively be used. Officers on the bridge were able to see the status of individual navigation lights as they were replicated on a panel on the bridge and bulbs showed when lights were on and illuminated, or had failed.

Floodlights illuminated the smoke stacks and areas of the ship, these lights were placed on the Compass Platform and on top of the deck games locker and Main Lounge dome, as well as on the after side of the bridge wings.

Signal Flags

A cabinet full of signaling flags was kept on the Bridge, these were attached to the mast and used to display messages to other ships as needed, or observers on the shore.

(Above) Signal flags hang high from the foremast.

The *Queen Mary* also displayed the Civil Ensign of the United Kingdom, a flag indicating she was a British ship, being registered in Liverpool, England (Liverpool was displayed in big capital letters on the aft end of the ship and originally on her lifeboats).

Keeping a Good Lookout

At 1,019 ft. 6 in. long and taking up to ten miles to stop, it was important for officers to be able to see around the *Queen Mary* at all times, here are some of design features that enabled them to do so.

Clear View Screens

Rain, spray and snow was thrown off the 'Clear View' screens (two of the Bridge's windows) by the centrifugal force of a rotating glass disc, resulting in a clear view outside in these conditions.

Crow's Nest

Lookouts climbed one hundred and ten steps inside the foremast to reach the crow's nest (entrance to the mast was on B Deck). The nest gave an elevated view from 130 ft. above sea level and had electric heaters, a steel hood and a glass weather screen.

Bridge Wings

Deck Officers had an unobstructed view along the sides of the ship from Bridge Wings that extended 12 ft. beyond the side of the ship.

(Above) Port Bridge Wing showing the ingenious air slot along the top edge of the wing.

To protect deck officers from the harsh elements air was driven up and over the Bridge wing by the addition of a high-pressure air slot on the front of the wing which accelerated the oncoming air.

Docking Bridge

The Docking Bridge was located at the aft end of the Promenade Deck. Officers were able to assist docking from the raised platform with a clear view of the ship's stern. They could also receive steering commands from the Wheelhouse on a telegraph positioned in the middle of the Docking Bridge.

(Above) Looking aft, the Docking Bridge.

The ship could be steered from a room underneath the center portion of the Docking Bridge (accessed from the Main Deck) which was considered a wheel house, it had a steering telegraph, compass, wheel and telephone.

Submarine Signals

Submarine signals warned the crew of approaching vessels, and gave direction of lightships.

173

Radar

A medium range surface-search radar was installed towards the end of World War II, in 1942. It was mounted behind the Compass Platform on a water tank.

Later in the post-war refit the unit was replaced with a smaller radar.

(Above) Radar on Compass Platform above Bridge.

Conversion Notes: The radar on the Compass Platform now is not functional. The wooden steps that led to the Compass Platform have been removed.

Fire Protection

Fire safety was engineered into the ship with fireproof bulkheads dividing the ship, fire doors and fire proof treatment of wooden surfaces in public rooms.

Handheld foam extinguishers, pressurized water hoses (18,780 ft. in total) and automatic sprinklers were available to fight fires.

(Above) Fire equipment exhibition.

Additionally there was a CO_2 extinguishing plant on E Deck for all non-accessible spaces. Air from these spaces was drawn through a Richaudio Smoke Detection Cabinet

(Lux-Rich) that used a light beam to illuminate smoke and a photo-electric system alarm that would have rang a gong.

A fire station was located towards the bow of the ship on C Deck (now R Deck) adjacent to the cabins of fire patrol men, who regularly patrolled the ship. There was an additional fire station on D Deck. A 7 ft. by 7 ft. fire panel had nearly three hundred lights on outlines of the ship's decks that would have shown the location of a fire.

(Above) Fire panel with indicator lights on deck plans.

Double Bottomed Hull

SHIP WITHIN A SHIP

The hull had a double-bottom that ran the full length of the ship and extended up the sides of the ship in places by nearly 40 ft. (illustrated on page 13). The space in-between the outer and inner shells was almost 6 ft. and this area was also split into nearly one hundred and sixty watertight compartments.

Should the ship run aground or the outer hull be compromised by an accident, the inner hull was intended to keep the ship water tight.

Watertight Doors & Bulkheads

Should an accident occur the ship was protected against flooding by eighteen transverse watertight bulkheads on to which water tight doors were installed. There were thirty eight power-controlled sliding doors (thirty four operated vertical and four horizontally) that could be sealed on command from the Bridge in under one minute. These doors were up to 6' 8" high and 5' wide. There were also twenty eight hinged type doors.

Once activated from a master control panel on the Bridge a bell at each hydraulic door rang out indicating they were going to close in seven seconds time.

(Above) Hydraulic door master control panel on the Bridge.

(Above) Hydraulic door exhibit on the *Queen Mary*.

The doors moved under 700 lbs. per square inch pressure which was provided by two steam driven hydraulic pressure pumps located in the aft Turbo-Generator Room.

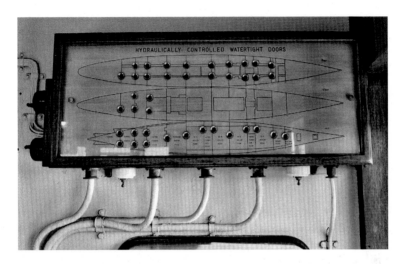

(Above) Panel in the Bridge showing position of the water tight hydraulic doors by illuminating lights.

Lights illuminated on a panel in the Bridge (shown above) when the hydraulic doors were closed, indicating the position of all thirty eight doors to the officers.

Once closed, the doors could withstand 30 tons of pressure and still remain watertight.

John Pedder, a young fireman on the ship was crushed to death in 1966 by door #13 during a fire drill.

Conversion Notes: Door #13 is located on the starboard side of H Deck (now G Deck) in Shaft Alley. The door is now permanently secured open.

Lifeboats

Twenty four steel lifeboats were positioned above the Sun Deck and readily available if needed to abandon ship. They had a total capacity of three thousand two hundred and sixty six persons, more than the passengers and crew onboard.

Number and capacity of lifeboats:

Type	Number	Size	Capacity (Total)
Motor Lifeboat	20	36'	145 (2,900)
Motor Lifeboat (with Wireless)	2	36'	136 (272)
Motor Lifeboat (Accident Boats)	2	30'	47 (94)

The lifeboats were fitted with a 18 B.H.P. two-cylinder diesel engine and a 21-gallon fuel tank, they were capable of 6 knots. Some supplies were kept onboard such as bread, water and condensed milk.

The lifeboats sat high above the Sun Deck and were hooked on to cradles, the cradles sat perched on top of davits (the brackets mounted to the deck). These cradles were secured to stop them sliding off but were ready to slide down tracks when the brake was released, by gravity or winch. Unlike earlier ships like the *Titanic*, the *Queen*

Mary's lifeboats could be lowered by one person. When the cradle reached a certain point the bracket pivoted to position the lifeboat alongside inward opening gates on the Sun Deck (to prevent accidental opening) permitting access to the lowered lifeboats. Boat lowering lights were at each boat station.

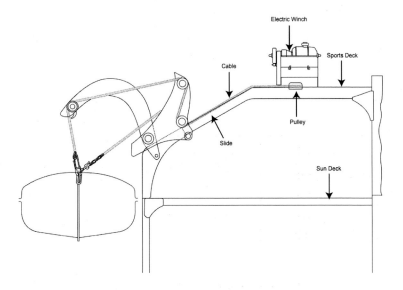

(Above) Lifeboat in lowered position.

(Above) Inward opening gate on the Sun Deck, which would have provided rapid access to a lowered lifeboat.

The 18 3/4 ton lifeboats could be winched back onto the davits by electrically driven winches which were positioned on the adjacent catwalks.

Lifeboat Inventory

15 ft. oars	5
boat hooks	2
axes	2
fire extinguishers	2
spirit compass with lamp	1
canvas anchor	1
bailer	1
brass lamp and gallon of oil	1
gallon of storm oil in perforated bag	1
tin of distress flares	1
matches	1
toolbox	1
life lines	-
quart of fresh water per passenger	-
1 lb. tin of condensed milk per passenger	-
21 lbs. of biscuits per passenger	-

Conversion: Two of the lifeboats are missing, #24 and #25. The lifeboats used to be covered by tarps but they are gone and the lifeboats exposed to the elements.

Life Jackets

Located around the ship were three thousand three hundred Boddy-Finch life jackets, they were made from cotton cloth filled with Java kapok (fibrous vegetable material honeycombed with air cells) and each weighed approximately 2 lbs.

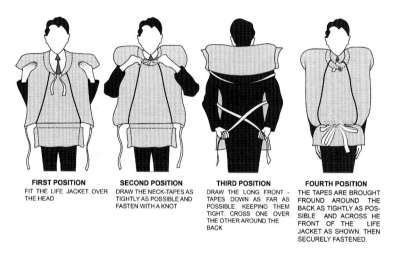

FIRST POSITION
FIT THE LIFE JACKET OVER THE HEAD

SECOND POSITION
DRAW THE NECK-TAPES AS TIGHTLY AS POSSIBLE AND FASTEN WITH A KNOT

THIRD POSITION
DRAW THE LONG FRONT - TAPES DOWN AS FAR AS POSSIBLE. KEEPING THEM TIGHT. CROSS ONE OVER THE OTHER AROUND THE BACK

FOURTH POSITION
THE TAPES ARE BROUGHT FROUND AROUND THE BACK AS TIGHTLY AS POSSIBLE AND ACROSS HE FRONT OF THE LIFE JACKET AS SHOWN. THEN SECURELY FASTENED.

(Above) Life jacket instructions.

Life Preservers

Thirty life preservers (life buoys) were attached to the upper railings and most had an attached electric light.

185

Conclusion

For over eighty years the *RMS Queen Mary* has amazed, breaking records during construction and throughout her life at sea, saving countless lives during the war, and still proudly welcoming all who visit.

(Above) *RMS Queen Mary* proudly docked in Long Beach, Ca.

Retired longer than she operated, as predicted by Lady Mable Fortescue-Harrison in 1934 she truly knows her greatest fame and popularity when she never sailed another mile.

Credits & Image Copyright

Bibliography

The Cunard White Star Quadruple-Screw Liner
Guide to Accommodation, Cunard White Star
The Queen Mary, Her Early Years Recalled
Weekly Illustrated Special "Queen Mary"